IMAGES
of Scotland

BROUGHTY FERRY

Happy 60TH Birthday
Dad.
Time to reminisce.
with Love from
Lynn & Best
xxxx

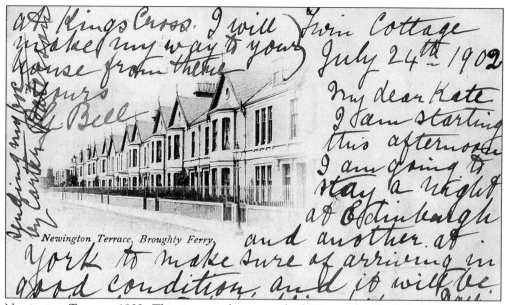

Newington Terrace, Broughty Ferry,

Handwritten text on postcard: "at Kings Cross. I will make my way to your house from there. yours G. Bell. Twin Cottage July 24th 1902. My dear Kate I am starting this afternoon I am going to stay a night at Edinburgh and another at York to make sure of arriving in good condition, and it will be"

Newington Terrace, 1902. This is an early postcard of BF sent by G. Bell, Twin Cottage, Church Street, to Kate Keiller in London, notifying her of his planned visit. Around this time telephones had only been installed in a few of the large houses in BF. Sarah Gilroy, widow of George Gilroy, must have been one of the first, as her telephone number was BF4. The increasingly popular, cheap alternative form of rapid communication was the postcard. With four collections on Mondays to Fridays, three on Saturdays and regular deliveries, local postcards sent in the morning could arrive on the afternoon of the same day.

Brook Street, Broughty Ferry.

Handwritten text on postcard: "The hymn-book arrived on Saturday morning I thank you for sending it on. I have had rather a busy time since I came home, and haven't written much, but we will be doing so some night soon, I hope you are enjoying the lovely weather we are having here just now. hoping you are all well with love from both Inemaui"

Brook Street, 1902. This early card has been sent by Miss Watson to her sister in Dunfermline. Each of these two early postcards has a small picture area with space for the message to be written alongside. The reverse of the card was kept for the address only. In 1902 the divided back was introduced, whereby the message and address could be written on the reverse of the postcard. However not all publishers changed over immediately. Valentine and Sons Ltd, Dundee, had changed at least by September 1902.

IMAGES
of Scotland

BROUGHTY FERRY

Compiled by
Andrew Cronshaw

TEMPUS

First published 1998
Copyright © Andrew Cronshaw, 1998

Tempus Publishing Limited
The Mill, Brimscombe Port,
Stroud, Gloucestershire, GL5 2QG

ISBN 0 7524 1509 3

Typesetting and origination by
Tempus Publishing Limited
Printed in Great Britain by
Midway Clark Printing, Wiltshire

Comic postcard, *c.* 1919. Since BF was a popular seaside resort, there was a wide range of comic postcards available. This card was published by Miller and Lang, Glasgow, but many were issued by Valentine, R.Tuck & Sons Ltd and others. However, the aim of this book has been to concentrate on the topographical postcards of BF.

Contents

CASTLE AND HARBOUR, BROUGHTY FERRY. 1207

A group of school children gather to catch the next boat, *c.* 1912.

Introduction

Broughty Ferry grew from a fishing community clustered around a harbour and protected by a castle. By the late 1830s, middle-class residents had begun to migrate across from Dundee and the opening of the Dundee and Arbroath Railway, in 1838, made visiting and commuting possible. Broughty Ferry provided these former townspeople with an opportunity for a quieter life and more spacious housing, with an escape from compact city tenements. The clean sea air was far healthier than the city's pollution, caused by domestic coal fires, factory chimneys and, on certain days, the processing carried out at Keiller's marmalade and confectionery works in the centre of Dundee. Broughty also provided a safer environment in which to escape from outbreaks of infectious diseases.

In the 1840s and 1850s, most of the town was situated south of Queen Street and laid out according to General Charles Hunter of Burnside's neat gridiron plan. By the 1860s and 1870s, many of the elite industrial upper class in Dundee had moved to 'the Ferry' and built large villas on the rising land behind the town. Construction of houses also extended from Dundee for some three and a half miles along the north bank of the Firth of Tay. The proprietors of Dundee's textile firms normally owned the grandest and most lavishly decorated mansions. Broughty also attracted lawyers, doctors, churchmen, professors and men who had retired from the Services. During the construction of the second Tay Bridge, a few younger men stayed. Whilst these developments took place, the Broughty fishing industry, after peaking in the 1880s, went into a period of decline. The introduction of new technology and methods brought an end to their traditional lifestyle.

The population of Broughty Ferry rose from 2,782 in 1851 to 7,407 in 1891. By the turn of the century, this figure had reached 10,500 and this number increased by half as many again during the summer months when visitors came to holiday in the area. By 1900, Broughty was said to be the wealthiest suburb in Britain. Some people made the exaggerated claim that there were more millionaires per square mile than in any settlement of comparable size. Certainly, in the exclusive parts there was street after street of grand houses, surrounded by well-kept grounds, conservatories, stables and lodges. Some of these mansions surpassed many of Scotland's country houses in their size and splendour. There was fierce competition between the resident jute manufacturing families. Carbet Castle, the home of the Grimmonds, expanded in an eccentric style to match the size of rival Castleroy, the home of the Gilroys. Unfortunately, neither mansion has survived today, each having suffered from terminal dry rot and neglect.

In 1864, Broughty Ferry became a police burgh. In 1913, Dundee, after a period of indecision, proposed to annex Broughty Ferry. The fishing community saw that their livelihood and identity would disappear and the jute barons became very concerned about the imposition of city rates and falling property values. There was intense opposition to the intended merger led by the Earl of Home and Alexander Bruce Gilroy. In November 1913, Broughty Ferry appealed against the unification in the House of Lords but lost the case and the town became part of the city, making Dundee the third largest city in Scotland at that time.

For several decades the affluent jute barons and their families enjoyed an exceptional standard of living. They were geographically separated from the harsh realities of city life experienced by the majority of Dundee residents. In spite of their large houses, the size of the merchants' families were often small. Some of the sons were so wealthy that they were able to enjoy a life of leisure and live off private means. Many descendants of wealthy families never married and when they died a very artificial and priviledged lifestyle, supported by all their domestic servants, came to an abrupt end. When Miss Betty Gilroy, sister of David R. Gilroy, died, there was a two-day auction sale of the contents of Rowanbank. The sale took place on the 20 and 21 November 1923. Exceptional items for sale at this five-bedroomed house included: a very valuable rosewood boudoir grand piano by J. Broadwood & Sons, an oak billiard table, a fine hall clock, a pedestal writing table, pictures, furniture, china, crystal and silverware. Since the size of a prosperous family was often small, the children usually received the best education that money could buy and many were clearly very able. Charles Edward Gilroy, the second son of Alexander Gilroy, entered Harrow in 1883. Five years later, he gained a place in the school cricket eleven and played against Eton at Lords. Charles also became captain of Harrow football team for a season. After receiving this privileged education, he became a partner in Gilroy, Sons & Co. Ltd and continued to play cricket for Forfarshire. Many prominent Broughty residents supported the local community. The work and influence of Alexander Bruce Gilroy and James Guthrie Orchar are described in later chapters.

Today, the 'Ferry' remains an attractive spot in which to live and there is still a quiet feeling of prosperity and individuality as you wander in and out of the shops and down the side streets. Unlike Dundee, Broughty has managed to escape massive redevelopment. There has been a realisation in the town that careful planning must be carried out in order to preserve the character of the area. In 1984, the last remaining section of Carbet Castle was demolished as part of the proposed building of twenty-nine houses on the plot. However, the Scottish Office blocked their construction. In August 1997, a new fifteen flat development, designed with the original building in mind and in conjunction with Historic Scotland, was begun. The new building, with its towers and spires, should meet with traditionalist approval when it is completed.

Throughout this book Broughty Ferry is referred to as 'Broughty', the 'Ferry' or, for the sake of further compactness the abbreviations 'BF' for Broughty Ferry and 'WF' for West Ferry have been used.

The majority of illustrations used in this book are from old picture postcards. The earliest cards of Broughty date from 1901 and are published by G.W. Wilson & Co. of Aberdeen. However, many more postcards of the town were published by Valentine & Sons Ltd, Dundee, and date from 1903 until the late 1960s. The early cards were collotyped in black and white before colour-printing methods were developed. However Rotary Photographic Co. Ltd, West Drayton introduced the first real photographic postcards to Great Britain in August 1901. Protected by patents, it was not until around 1907 that other publishers, such as Valentines, were able to produce their own real photographic topographical postcards. J.B. White Ltd, of Dundee used Rotary Photographic Co. Ltd, as a printer for their sepia postcards during the 1920s and frequently thereafter. The Edwardian postcard-collecting craze started gaining momentum around 1903, and postcard production peaked in about 1906. There were several small local stationers and postcard publishers who issued black and white, colour and real photographic postcards. These included Alexander Bowman, Brook Street, BF; David Dempster, Gray Street, BF; Robert H. Lundie Co, Reform Street, Dundee; and Shaw, King Street, BF. There were at least forty early publishers of BF postcards, most of which are represented in this volume.

In spite of the diversity of publishers, most visitors did not venture very far, and consequently most of the cards found are views of the harbour, castle and beach. The pictures chosen for this book have deliberately emphasised the scarcer subjects and rarer images found. Occasionally, certain key buildings have not been found represented on postcards. This may be due to rarity or the fact that they never existed in postcard form. Notable absences are the Southern and Western Public Schools and St Luke's church. Research has shown that Valentine and Sons Ltd or J.B. White Ltd did not publish these buildings on cards. The location of these buildings may have been too remote or well hidden in the case of the Southern School. However, for completeness, some historical notes relating to these establishments have been included in the text.

Whilst photographers supplied the Edwardian postcard publishers with a comprehensive set of still images of villages, towns and cities in Scotland and England, such a record of contemporary life is not available for future generations. It is important to go out, record and take good still photographs today, as townscapes and lifestyles continue to change in unforeseen ways.

Andrew Cronshaw
Edinburgh, May 1998

Acknowledgements

For their apt comments and suggestions, I would like to thank Lydia Catto, Nancy Davey, Iain Flett, Caroline Jackson, John M. Hunter, Revd Gordon D. Jamieson, Avril Lansdell, Charlotte Lythe, Revd Alan H. MacKay, Charles McKean and Jim Russell. I also acknowledge the Whitcombe Collection, Science Museum, London, for the tram photograph on p.93 (top).

My apologies for any inadvertent omissions in attribution.

One
West Ferry

West Ferry Bay, 1920. West Ferry became the western suburb of BF as the two areas expanded. BF started off as a small fishing village and in 1794 had a population of just 230. With the arrival of the Dundee and Arbroath Railway, the population in 1841 had grown to 1,980. Prosperity in Dundee in the nineteenth century caused the number of residents in BF to rise. The steady growth in the population of BF is shown in the census results of 1861, 1871, 1881, 1891 and 1901 as 3,513; 5,707; 7,407; 9,256 and 10,484 respectively. Today the component populations are West Ferry about 6,000, BF about 7,000 and Barnhill about 5,500.

The Grassy Beach, *c.* 1926. On the left is the timber framed Royal Tay Yacht Club, Beach Clubhouse. The notice pinned to the inside of one of the open doors advertised the Annual Regatta at West Ferry Bay. The Royal Tay Yacht Club was established in Dundee as the Tay Corinthian Sailing Club in 1885. In 1887 the club moved to premises at West Ferry Bay. In 1955 the club acquired nearby Fort William House, 34 Dundee Road, as their clubhouse.

Yacht Club Houses and beach, 1949. BF attracted many of Dundee's businessmen as the place to live. Douglas C. Thomson, the newspaper publisher, lived at Inveraron, West Ferry. In May 1886 Douglas, aged twenty-five, was in charge of his father's recently acquired newspaper business. Douglas continued to work in the *Courier* office until about six weeks before his death on 13 October 1954, aged ninety-three. As a pioneer motorist he owned one of the first motor cars in the district – a six-horsepower DeDion. Douglas was also an enthusiastic photographer and cine camera owner and one time President of Dundee Cine Society.

West Ferry Beach, c. 1903. On the morning after the Tay Bridge disaster much of the debris was washed up on West Ferry Beach. Wreckage from the carriages and bridge were taken to BF station yard whilst personal effects were taken to Dundee where they were displayed for relatives of the missing passengers to identify.

West Ferry Beach, c. 1903. On the morning after the Tay Bridge disaster several mail bags from the train were washed up on the beach. The letters were sorted and delivered that day as if no accident had occurred. In the morning the distressed postmistress in BF had sent a telegram to the Postmaster at the Dundee Central Post Office, informing and confirming the news of the accident.

Victoria Road, northward, 1906. Tram car No. 3, bound for BF and Monifeith, is about to turn into Albert Road. The tram route ran along Strathern Road, Victoria Road, Albert Road, Claypots Road and into Queen Street, which led to Monifeith Road. The large house beyond the gateposts is Aystree, designed in 1903. Aystree originally had a lodge, coach house and stables. Today, the house has multiple occupancy.

Harecraigs Brae, 1914. The open top motor car has an Aberdeen registration number, SR 60. Cars registered in Dundee used the registration letters TS and YJ. Registration number plates for motor cars and motor cycles were introduced in January 1904. Between 1914 and 1922, petrol cost about two shillings a gallon of which eight pence (33%) was tax. It was not until 1935 that the driving test was made compulsory.

Strathearn Terrace, West Ferry. 79001. J.V.

Strathern Terrace, eastward, 1914. On the right, tramcar No. 26 with a covered top, was bound for the High Street, Dundee. This real photographic postcard was published by Valentine and Sons Ltd, Dundee. Valentines started publishing postcards in the late 1890s. The firm issued their first real photographic postcards in May 1907. Valentines stopped publishing black and white postcards in 1967 and colour postcards in 1970.

Louise Terrace, West Ferry. J V 75392

Louise Terrace, northward, 1913. The cambered, compressed ground road surface was most suitable for horse drawn-vehicles. At this time motor cars were still a rare form of transport. The end of the road is clearly indicated by a line of about ten rows of cobblestones. This feature can be detected in other pictures in the look. The kerbstones mark the edge of an earth and gravel pavement and support the cobbled gutter system. Unmade pavements remain today in some of the residential parts of BF.

West Ferry Post Office, *c.* 1910. West Ferry Post Office opened as a town sub office on 17 January 1898. The P.O. became a money order and savings bank office on 1 March 1898. Postal orders had been introduced in 1881 as a cheaper alternative to money orders and could be bought and cashed at money order offices. The old county name of Forfarshire, often encountered in postmarks, changed to Angus on 25 July 1928. The early motor car shown in the photograph has a Dundee registration number, TS 28.

Dundee Road, eastward 1913. On the far left is an early road sign that indicated the maximum permitted speed limit of ten mph. On the right the spire and the roof of St Stephen's Established church can be seen. Also on the right are two horse-drawn delivery carts.

14

Two
The Fishing
Community

Fisher Street, *c.* 1904 The fishing community was located in a very compact area of BF. This was situated along Fisher Street, by the shore, and in an area just to the north, between Church Street and Gray Street. The fisherman's cottages were small but they often housed large families. In 1891 James and Mary Massie of 9 Fisher Street had three sons and five daughters aged between seventeen and four. Overcrowding was made worse as storage space had to be found for fishing nets and equipment. The kitchens were also small but were kept spotlessly clean. Space was found on the walls and shelves to display shining china and ornaments as a feature. St James church, 5 Fort Street, shown here, was formerly the Fisherman's Reading Room. The congregation was formed as Beach Established church in 1889. The church hall was added in 1907.

The Beach, Broughty Ferry

The Beach, c. 1907. The sail-fishing era in BF lasted at least from the 1790s until the late 1920s. The peak period for the BF fisherman was in the early 1880s when the fleet consisted of over eighty boats, which provided employment for about 180 men. Herring and white fish (plaice and haddock) were the main catches. The herring were caught off Aberdeen and Peterhead. The white fish were generally caught in areas around St Andrews Bay and Carnoustie Bay.

The Harbour, c. 1907. In the 1790s the fishing community consisted of a few fisherman's huts situated along the shore to the west of today's Gray Street. The men fished with lines for flounder, haddock and plaice, and with nets for herring. At this time the fishermen used three large fishing boats.

The Beach, Broughty Ferry

The Beach, *c.* 1907. The building on the left is the Beach Established church founded in 1889. The first low cottage, to the right of the church, was built for the Bell family in 1812. In 1859 a barometer in a box was attached to the right side of the doorway of this typical fisherman's cottage. Barometer Cottage, as it became known, has since lost the barometer, presented by the Meteorological Society, but the long case remains. In the centre of the picture fishing nets can be seen drying in the sun.

Beach Crescent, Broughty Ferry

The Beach, *c.* 1907. By 1845 the fishing fleet had grown to approximately thirteen open boats, each with a crew of about six men. The fishing boats set off either at night or in the early morning. Fishing at night was very cold work as the boats had no heating. In the spring and winter the men went white fishing. In the summer the fishermen ventured north to the herring grounds of Peterhead.

At Pier Head, c. 1909. By 1855 BF had seventy-six fishermen and a fleet of thirty boats. Ten of the boats were over thirty feet long, fourteen boats were between eighteen and thirty feet long and six boats were less than eighteen feet long. Most were open boats that could be hauled ashore. On the left was William Reid's Refreshment Rooms at 45 Fisher Street. This was a restaurant and not a public house.

At the beach, c. 1909. In the 1860s larger deep sea trawlers were introduced to the fleet. By 1873 the fishing boats had acquired steam capstans to haul in the drift nets. By 1882 the number of trawlers had increased to about twenty. The invasion of the more popular and efficient steam and motor trawlers caused problems for the other fisherman that preferred traditional techniques. The line fishermen could not compete with the trawlers and in order to survive were forced further out to sea, which was more dangerous.

Lifeboat house, Fisher Street at the foot of Fort Street, *c.* 1909. In 1830 a lifeboat was acquired by public subscription after a series of shipwrecks and located at Buddon Ness. The boat was equipped with twelve rowing and two steering oars and space for twenty to thirty men. The location, however, was inconvenient for BF crewmembers. By 1859 a second lifeboat was acquired and moored off BF. On 19 December 1861, the RNLI took over the BF lifeboat station and a lifeboat shed was built at the foot of Fort Street. In 1909 a new lifeboat house and slip was built on the site of the old lifeboat shed. In May 1935 a new motor lifeboat called *Mona*, capable of carrying 120 persons, was installed as a result of an anonymous donation. On 8 December 1959 the *Mona* was called out to a rescue in severe weather and capsized. Her eight-crew members were drowned. In 1962 a memorial plaque was placed on the outside of the lifeboat station in remembrance of the tragedy.

On the Beach, *c*. 1905. By 1871 BF had 110 fishermen, which increased to 180 fishermen in 1881. In 1881 there were over eighty boats in the BF area. This was the peak period for the local fishing industry. The fleet decreased to seventy-five in 1891 and to fifty in 1901. In spite of the arrival of the trawlers, BF fishermen failed to equip their fishing boats with motors when they were introduced in 1906. Further decline occurred when herring fishing by trawlers became confined to ports, which had deep water at all states of the tide. A fisherman is shown inspecting and untangling a fishing line and perhaps removing bait or replacing missing hooks.

Boiling whelks, *c*. 1905. The fishermen's cottages in the background are in Fisher Street to the west of the lifeboat house. Whelks were boiled in large cauldrons on the beach. When catches of fish were poor, especially towards the end of the nineteenth century, periwinkles (whelks, wilks) were collected and boiled for sale. This is one of a series of six postcards published by Raphael Tuck and Sons Ltd, London.

Study of fisher life, *c*. 1905. The fisherman's wives have gathered on the shore to socialise and wash clothes. Another of the wives' tasks was to obtain bait and attach it to the fishing lines. The commonest type of bait was lugworm found locally near Barnhill and Buddon Ness. Bait was dug with special long-handled spades and taken to BF. The women would then bait the lines, each of which could contain over 700 hooks. Loading the bait was sometimes carried out at midnight. Other types of bait included rigger-worm and mussels.

Fisher Life, *c*. 1905. Most fishermen brought boats new or second-hand from yards or fishermen in Montrose, Arbroath or Anstruther. The most common Scottish fishing boat used for line and net fishing was the yawl usually of the 'Fifie' class. These were smaller than the larger herring boats. Most small boats carried a single lugsail on a fore mast. The larger boats had fore and aft masts each with lugsails and occasionally a jib.

Fisher Life, Fisher Street, c. 1905. A fisherman's wife is seen knitting after pegging up the daily washing. Before long fishing journeys in the summer to the northern herring grounds, nets and equipment had to be repaired. Periodically the fishermen would 'bark' their nets, sails and lines by boiling them in large tubs of water containing wood bark. After this preservation process the nets and sails, which turned dark brown, were taken by cart to dry in fields behind BF. Several floats are seen drying alongside the washing on the line. Originally floats were made from animal bladders coated in oil.

At the beach, 1896. A young boy is seen mending fishing nets and two young women are shelling mussels. Fisherwomen wore large aprons to protect their clothes when gutting fish and baiting lines. On market days when selling fish, the same women wore distinctive, colourful, traditional skirts, petticoats and shawls to attract the attention of customers.

Broughty Ferry from the Old Pier

BF from the Old Pier, 1903. In the 1890s several trawling companies were formed in Dundee. They placed orders for modern steel trawlers with local shipyards. The local fishermen had to change with the times and find employment on Dundee trawlers. The wives, sons and daughters of the fishermen found more secure employment in the Dundee factories and mills or became domestic servants in Broughty's large houses. As a consequence the BF fishing community began to decline.

Castle and beach, c. 1906. This fine composition, by an unknown photographer, shows the unloading of a catch on a very calm day. Behind the large anchor, a fisher lady waits with an empty creel. By 1928 the fleet, which still relied on sails, had been reduced to twelve boats, which employed thirty men. By 1948 the fleet had declined to four boats which employed just six men. Gradually the tradition of fishing died out and a tough way of life came to an end.

HOME FROM THE FISHING ON THE TAY.   1202

Fishermen returning, *c.* 1912. When the catches arrived the fish had to be sorted and sold. The main market was the fish market, at the Greenmarket, Shore Terrace, Dundee. The fishwives sold fish on Tuesdays, Fridays and Saturdays. With no refrigeration, the condition of the fish often deteriorated. *The BF fisherwomen had to walk to and from Dundee with their creels of fish each market day.* In 1891 there were specialist occupations of fisherman, fish dealers and fish saleswomen within the Fisher Street community.

Morning at the Beach, Broughty Ferry.   73924 JV.

Morning at the beach, *c.* 1912. The fisherman's catch was unloaded into a horse-drawn cart in the shallow waters of the bay. In the 1830s BF catches could not supply the demand for fish in Dundee as great quantities of fish were brought to the city from Fife. In addition some women travelled all the way from Auchmithie with crabs, lobsters and dried fish in their creels. By 1912 Dundee trawlers landed most (89%) of the fish for local consumption. A further 11% of fresh and cured fish was brought in by rail.

Unloading boats, *c*. 1912. Once a catch was brought ashore it was auctioned to the fish buyers or taken to Dundee to be sold. The flat fish were often barrelled locally and sent to Liverpool or Manchester. The herring were sent to Arbroath or Montrose for smoking and curing. In 1912 Dundee trawlers landed 3,800 tons of fish. On the dockside in Dundee, the Ice and Cold Storage Company manufactured twenty-five tons of ice daily. Clarence Birdseye invented deep-freezing in America in 1923 and frozen foods were first retailed in Springfield, Massachussetts in 1930.

Evening scene, *c*. 1913. This picture was taken after the boats had been unloaded. The stationers, Davidson and Son, Kirkcaldy, published the postcard. John Davidson (1811 – 1887) founded the firm in 1840 when John established a newsagents shop in Linktown. Within the shop John set up a newspaper reading club which proved popular. By 1850 John had moved to the High Street, Kirkcaldy. Davidson's son, John Davidson junior, became a partner in the business in 1882 and became involved in printing in 1896. John Davidson junior died on 1 August 1923. The firm continued to flourish after this date but no longer published postcards. Davidson and Son published many postcards of Scotland, certainly from 1907 to 1917.

Broughty Castle and Harbour.

Castle and Harbour, *c.* 1904. In 1866 an epidemic of cholera swept the country. In BF the disease was most prevalent in the fishing community and quickly caused twelve deaths. The outbreak brought pressure to close the Old Burial Ground, Chapel Lane, off Fisher Street. The closure on 25 May 1867 brought protests from the fishing community even though as a compromise a further fourteen old people were allowed to be buried there. William Skirving, the 70-year-old local gravedigger, continued secretly to open up graves after this date. In August 1867 William was caught making an illegal burial and fined £5. The local fisherman jointly paid the fine and made William Skirving a hero. In 1869 Barnhill cemetery opened and the troubles at the Old Burial Ground ended. The cholera outbreak was attributed to contamination of water drawn from wells. In 1869 a purer water supply was authorised to be supplied to BF under the Dundee Water Act. This fine Art Nouveau style postcard was one of a short series published by a local stationer, David Dempster, 101 Gray Street.

Three
The Beach

Children's Corner, 1913. The seaside holiday in Britain began as a craze for medicinal sea bathing in the mid-eighteenth century. The trend spread from the landed gentry to the prosperous middle classes. In time visitors from lower down the social scale were able to make journeys to resorts, stay longer and spend more. Increasingly people were able to stay for an extra day or two, if times were good, and go away for the whole Trades holiday. Certainly by the 1830s BF had become a fashionable seaside resort for the better off. It was some decades later before BF attracted industrial workers from Dundee in large numbers. Families also travelled from further afield. Visitors came from Perth and Glasgow during their official holiday periods. BF offered miles of sandy beaches, a promenade, bathing, boat excursions, bowling, golf, bandstand music, pierrots and later on an art gallery.

Beach crescent and castle, 1903. The second building on the left, from this photograph of 1921, was the Orchar Gallery named after Provost James Orchar. This large stone villa overlooking the harbour was built in 1866 for a member of the Stephen shipbuilding family in Dundee. In 1894 Dundee Shipbuilders Co. Ltd took over Alexander Stephen and Sons yard in Dundee and it was from this yard that RRS *Discovery* was launched in March 1901. Since the closure of the gallery the building has become the Orchar Nursing Home.

Beach Crescent, 1913. James Guthrie Orchar was born in 1925 and became provost of BF in 1887, a position he held for twelve years. On his death in 1898, James Orchar bequeathed money to house his fine collection of about 300 pictures gifted to all the citizens of the town. James Orchar had originally intended that the collection should be housed in a new gallery in Reres Park. However, the pictures were displayed in an existing building, the Orchar Gallery at 31 Beach Crescent from 1921.

Harbour Esplanade, Broughty Ferry.

Beach Crescent, *c.* 1928. James Orchar left an endowment for an extension to the gallery that opened on 13 September 1937, and for the purchase of new artwork. The collection of fine nineteenth century paintings contained pictures by Sir Henry Raeburn and Sir William MacTaggart. The gallery closed in 1980 after an electrical fire and the collection was moved to the McManus Galleries, Albert Square, Dundee in 1982.

Broughty Ferry, Castle and Windmill. 1855.

BF Windmill, *c.* 1850. A windmill once stood on the green outside the castle. The decline of the windmill began when steam power was applied to flour milling in 1850s. BF windmill was used last century by a local joiner who harvested the windpower to turn a lathe. Broughty castle can be seen in the distance before its restoration by the War Office in 1861. Certainly in 1643 Dundee possessed a windmill which stood westward of the packhouse at the lower end of the more recent Union Street. The packhouse was a large warehouse built on land reclaimed from the Tay.

Broughty Castle, *c.* 1905. Broughty Castle dates from around 1490. However, by the late 1780s the castle was a ruin. In 1846 the Edinburgh and Northern Railway Co. bought the castle to enable them to construct the rail ferry harbour terminal in conjunction with the Dundee and Arbroath Railway Co. Between 1849 and 1851 the harbour was designed by engineers Thomas Bouch and Thomas Grainger and constructed for the railway companies.

BF from the castle, looking north, *c.* 1905. In November 1854 the War Office bought the castle following fears that a Russian invasion was imminent. Reconstruction of the castle started in February 1860 and was completed by June 1861. Restoration was believed to be authentic but nothing above the first floor level is original. The castle became the HQ for the new 3rd (BF) Forfarshire Artillery Volunteers until 1870.

The Castle, Broughty Ferry.

B5177 JV.

Broughty Castle, 1921. Between 1888 and 1907 the castle was occupied again as a garrison HQ. This time by the Tay Division of Submarine Miners Royal Engineers (Volunteers). The role of the Volunteers was to protect the navigable channels of the Tay estuary by laying mines. A railway line was used to push mines along the pier in trolleys. At the end of the pier a small crane lifted the mines into small launches. The mines were then located at various depths in the Tay estuary. The mines could be retrieved again using a hoist on the steam launch.

View from the castle, c. 1955. During the First World War, the Royal Garrison Artillery Battery occupied the castle. In 1930 remaining members of the garrison left and the castle was declared an ancient monument. With the outbreak of the Second World War, the War Department garrisoned the castle with the 503 Coast Regiment Royal Artillery. However during both world wars the defences of the castle were never tested. In 1949 the castle was leased to Dundee Corporation who used it briefly as a tearoom. In 1969 the castle opened as a museum.

General View of Beach from the Battery, Broughty Ferry.

View of beach from the castle, 1920. The sandy shore sloped gradually into the Tay Estuary and provided safe bathing, as there was practically no current. In 1920 bathing machines were still in use, and they can be seen here at the waters edge, beyond the entertainers stage. In 1915 bathing coaches were available for hire at 3d per person. This also included the hire of a bathing costume and towel. Certainly by the 1930s a bathing station at the castle end of the Esplanade provided changing room space for visitors. The building on the left is the beach shelter.

Castle Terrace, Broughty Ferry

Castle Terrace, c. 1909. The visitor to Castle Terrace has indicated, with a cross on the postcard, the house in which he was staying. As holidaymakers in BF, tourists were by no means restricted to a beach holiday. Railway and sailing excursions were possible. There were steamer trips to St Andrews, Arbroath, Montrose and to the Bell Rock Lighthouse. Cruise trips were also available up the Tay to Newburgh and Perth. In 1939, at the time of war, the sea front along Castle Terrace was built up with sandbags, but no postcard showing this was published.

Newington Terrace, *c.* 1908. If a visitor wished to stay by the beach, Newington Terrace provided that opportunity. On Friday and Saturday evenings in the summer it was possible to take a cruise on the *Argyle* commanded by Captain Edwards. Around 1910 these circular trips from BF visiting Tayport and the Tay Bridge were very popular, with dancing on board. TS *Mars* was a training ship anchored in the Tay and used for the upbringing of deprived boys. The ship was a form of industrial school with a naval style of discipline.

Promenade, 1923. Before the Esplanade was laid out the area was a pleasant stretch of natural links. In 1894 the Esplanade, a favourite promenade which ran for nearly a mile along the shore, was constructed. As part of the Esplanade development at this time, a Swiss Chalet style tearoom, a shelter and a new bandstand were erected. Anticipating this development, Alexander Bowman, an enterprising local stationer, published a BF Annual for 1894, which provided a descriptive, illustrated guide for visitors.

The Seaside, c. 1915. Eight bathing machines and the horse used to draw them into the water can be seen. On the roofs of five of the machines are adverts for the Empress Laundry managed by Mrs Guild, 84 High Street, Dundee. The bathing machine was invented at Margate by Benjamin Beale, a Quaker in 1753, to enable women to bathe in seclusion. The user entered from the rear and undressed, while a horse pulled the machine down the beach into the sea. When the floor was just above the waves the swimmer could emerge discretely.

Beach, c. 1912. By the 1880s it was required that bathing costumes for men and women should cover them from neck to knee and be made of material that caused no indecent exposure when wet. Between 1880 and 1900 costumes were used for bathing only and not worn for sitting on the beach. In the late Victorian period, men usually wore a dark one-piece costume made of thin knitted cotton fabric. The costumes were hired out by the owners of the bathing machines. At this time women wore a one-piece combination suit with an overskirt.

On the Sands, 1923. The most popular times for bathing on a sunny day were between 11.00am and 12.30pm, and 3.00pm and 4.30pm. In the 1860s men and women bathed on different parts of the beach. The number of bathing machines in use were strictly controlled and licensed. By the early twentieth century there were a few changes, families could swim together; bathing machines were replaced by fixed beach huts situated above the high tide mark; and changing on the beach behind a canvas wind break or a towel was permitted.

Rowing Boats at BF, 1926. In May 1906 licences were granted for eight rowing boats at the beach and for nine ponies or donkeys. Rowing boat trips were very popular, but were later to be replaced by motor boats. A donkey ride along the beach cost 1d. Donkey rides had been introduced to English beaches in the 1850s and by the 1860s had become an established part of the seaside.

Promenade and seaside, *c*. 1932. From the time sea bathing began in Britain, male and female bathers had been segregated. In 1901 mixed bathing was permitted at Bexhill, East Sussex. By 1914 mixed bathing was almost universal and bathing machines gradually disappeared as people changed in huts or on the beach. Between 1900 and 1920 women's costumes changed more than men's. Women now wore closer fitting combinations without an overskirt similar in design to men's costumes. Costumes could still be hired from beach attendants.

Seaside, *c*. 1936. After the First World War it became fashionable to expose your skin to the sun for the first time. In 1911 swimming costumes were made from cotton stockinette and in the 1920s of machine – knitted wool. In the 1930s most men and women owned their own bathing costume. By the end of the 1930s a new elasticated fabric called Lastex was used for swimming costumes. Plain rubber bathing caps were worn by female swimmers to keep their hair dry, in the late 1920s.

36

Beach, c. 1928. In the 1920s men wore blazers, white flannel trousers with turn ups and open necked shirts. By the 1930s rolled up shirtsleeves were acceptable on the beach and short sleeved shirts and shorts were introduced. By 1930 the boater hat had disappeared and panama hats were only worn by older men. In the 1920s women wore cotton dresses with knitted jackets which were replaced by waist-length cardigans by the 1930s. Shorts and blouses were also worn on the beach.

Snap photographs taken on BF Beach, 1933. Three generations of a family are seen enjoying a few hours on the beach. The invention of roll film by George Eastman in 1888 enabled middle-class families to take their own holiday photographs. Daylight loading roll film became available in the late 1890s. In 1900 Eastman introduced the Kodak Box Brownie camera at the bargain price of five shillings. A year or so later the Number 2 Brownie was introduced which took $2 \frac{1}{4}$ x$3 \frac{1}{4}$ inch pictures. The photograph illustrated here was perhaps taken by an updated version of this model of camera. Certainly by the 1930s the Brownie camera had made photography accessible to all.

The beach, 1953. In the early 1950s BF continued to attract visitors. The driver of the coach has opened the top of his vehicle to keep the interior cool. On the waters edge a wooden observation platform for a lifesaver has been introduced. At this time motor cars were mainly available in a choice of two colours, grey or black. The local family seaside holiday tailed off during the 1950s and 1960s with the growth in car ownership, the building of motorways, the jet plane and the package tour.

The sands, c. 1955. Deck chairs first appeared on beaches for hire in the late 1890s. This form of hammock chair was originally made as camp furniture for the army in India in the 1870s. The chairs were later used on board ships, hence the name 'deckchair'. In the hey-day of Dundee's prosperity one of the sights visible from the beach was the arrival of tall, three-masted sailing ships with jute from India. Tugboats travelled out from Dundee to meet the ships and if the wind was in the right direction the sails remained inflated.

Four
Street Scenes

Brook Street, westward, *c.* 1902. Alexander Bowman, a prominent local stationer and publisher in Brook Street, was born in Montrose. He began his working life as a compositor for the *Montrose Review* and then a reporter, firstly for the *Review* and secondly for the *Dundee Courier*. Alex then joined the publishing office staff at the *Dundee Advertiser*. Around 1874 Alex started his own business as a stationer and bookseller in Brook Street but continued freelance work for the *Advertiser*, where for many years he was the local BF reporter. Certainly from 1894 Alex ran a circulating library from his shop. Books and magazines could be borrowed for 1d a night. In Dundee, stationer Robert Lundie also partitioned his shops to include a lending library section. Alex died on 11 August 1902 but the stationery business continued under his name. Bowman's the stationers published a few series of early postcards and periodically updated guide books of BF.

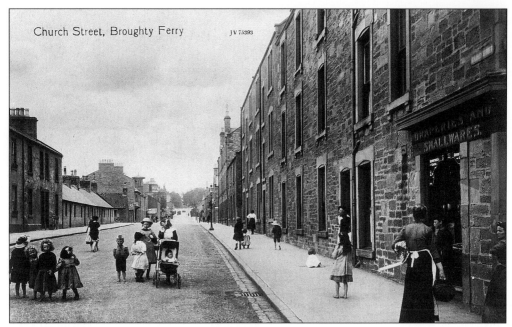

Church Street, Broughty Ferry   J V 75393

Church Street, northward, 1913. This is a fine animated view by a Valentine and Sons photographer. The shop on the right sold draperies and smallwares.

Church Street, southward, *c.* 1911. The building on the right was the West UF church hall. From the early 1890s, for the next two decades, there was a photographic portrait studio at Twin Cottages, Church Street.

Church Street and Grove Academy, Broughty Ferry.

Church Street and Grove Academy, *c.* 1913. The Volunteer Hall or Drill Hall, seen on the left, was built around 1875 for the 1st Forfarshire Artillery Volunteers (formed in 1860). The hall was also used as a venue for travelling theatre groups. Around 1900, pupils from the Beach School(Southern) put on a show of Gilbert and Sullivan's *HMS Pinafore*. In 1936 the hall was converted into the Regal Cinema. When the cinema closed in 1960 the building became the Kingsway Bingo Hall. Beyond the Hall is the Grove Academy. On the right are the two lower gas lamps attached to the taller electric street light, installed in 1902.

Seafield Road, northward, *c.* 1911. The message on the postcard sent on 26 July 1911 reads 'The Sunday School picnic did not come off, as it was a pouring wet day here, so Mr Begg gave each child sixpence on Coronation Day (22 June 1911) to make up for not having the picnic'. The land on the left is now occupied by newer buildings of Grove Academy.

Fort Street, *c.* 1908. The building on the left was the Union UF church. In 1846 the Gray family, the forerunner of Provost Baxter Gray, took over the running of the Fort Street Brewery, which had been in existance since the eighteenth century. The bridge seen in the distance replaced an earlier level crossing.

GRAY STREET LOOKING NORTH, BROUGHTY FERRY.   NO.

Gray Street, northward, *c.* 1912. The name 'Gray' was taken from Andrew, second Lord Gray, who resided at Broughty Castle in the late fifteenth century. The Gray family occupied the castle for the following 170 years.

Gray Street, northward, c. 1908. The main shopping area in BF since Victorian times was concentrated in Brook Street and King Street, particularly near the Gray Street intersections. This postcard was published by Alexander Bowman, stationer, Brook Street.

Gray Street, northward, c. 1903. This postcard was published by Valentine and Sons Ltd, Dundee. The majority of postcards of BF were by Valentines. As modes of transport changed and new buildings appeared, Valentines would update their postcard images.

Gray Street, northward, *c.* 1905. The site to the right of the horse and cart, beyond the arch and between the two lampposts, was developed in 1918 to provide the location for the BF Picture House. On the left, with the wall-mounted gaslight, was Jolly's Hotel, named after John Jolly, the owner.

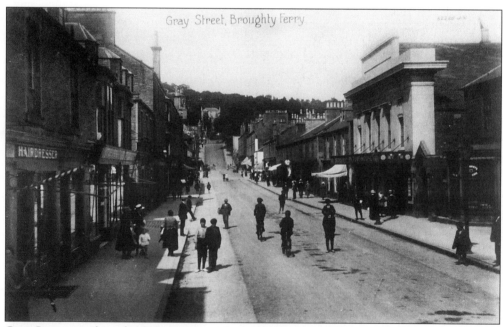

Gray Street, northward, 1919. On the right is the BF Picture House, which opened in 1918. The subject of the new cinema has been deliberately chosen by Valentine's photographer to convey a modern BF scene. Recently there has been a renewed interest in early films but unfortunately about 80 per cent of silent films have been lost.

Broughty Ferry Station, Gray Street, *c.* 1904. Around 1900 the stationmaster was a Mr Lamb, a tall and dignified gentleman with a grey beard. He always wore a tall hat and frock coat when on duty. Piled on seats at the entrance of the station each morning were two bundles of newspapers for the early morning trains. One pile contained the *Dundee Advertiser* priced one penny and the other the *Dundee Courier* priced one half-penny. On the left is an electric street light installed in 1902.

Gray Street, southward, *c.* 1938. This photograph was taken from the high signal box at BF station by Thomas White of J.B. White Ltd, Dundee. Many of White's real photographic sepia postcards were printed by Rotary Photographic Co. Ltd, West Drayton. Before the glass plates were sent to the printer the skies were often retouched using a brush.

45

St Vincent Street, northward, c. 1920. This postcard was published by an unknown firm and probably printed abroad.

St Vincent Street, c. 1908. Around 1900 a mussel boat from Taypoint regularly visited Broughty Beach. The mussels were loaded into a deep cart and transported to Broughty goods station. Water dripped from the cart all the way up St Vincent Street, passed the Eastern Public School. The old school is now used by St Aidan's Playgroup and the land opposite the school has been redeveloped to form the modern flats of St Vincent's Court.

St Vincent Street, northward, *c.* 1903. Castleroy, the home of George Gilroy's family is seen on the horizon. On the right stands the Eastern public school. East Queen Street UF church is seen on the left. The mansion in the trees below and to the left of Castleroy is Craig-gowan, built for James Mudie, steamship owner. The photograph is one of a series of images of BF, probably taken by local photographer Frank Gillies for G.W. Wilson and Co., Aberdeen.

Whinny Brae, northward, *c.* 1908. Heading northwards across Queen Street are situated some of BF's large houses, set in spacious grounds and often hidden by high walls, trees and hedges. Housework, and washing in days before time saving technology, was carried out by domestic servants, who worked to ordered daily routines. In Victorian times an upper-middle class family might have a butler, a lady's maid, a cook, a kitchen maid, a scullery maid and a laundry maid.

WHINNIE BRAE, BROUGHTY FERRY

Whinny Brae, southward, *c.* 1912. In the large houses household washing was given to a woman in a cottage to wash or to be done at home by servants. A Victorian family would have a large number of starched petticoats, children's frocks, garments with gofered frills, large tablecloths, sheets, napkins, towels, stiff shirts, collars and ties. This task would be carried out in three days by three to four maids in the washhouse-laundry area of a large home.

Oakley Place, northward, *c.* 1908. Sometimes the cook helped with the washing and a house-laundry maid would do other housework on non-laundry days. Sheets and tablecloths were ironed mechanically by wrapping them round the loose rollers of a huge box mangle. Conventional ironing was carried out by having irons stacked on three sides of a square stove which glowed red-hot. This meant there was always a hot iron ready for each maid to use. Fridays were mending days and three maids would sit sewing in the linen room all afternoon.

Hermitage Terrace, *c.* 1912. In 1851 one in nine of all females over the age of ten were employed as domestic servants. A young girl started as a kitchen maid; then she became a parlour maid or chambermaid; next she might progress to become a cook and eventually to a housekeeper. In 1901, 25 per cent of working women were employed in domestic service. By the 1930s the percentage had halved. Some of the large houses in BF had their own stables, coachmen and carriage. Not everyone however was so fortunate. In late Victorian times there was only one taxicab in the town. Consequently after parties people had to take the taxi in turns or share it.

Camphill Road, *c.* 1912. Camphill Road was the location for many large homes. In 1891 James Mudie employed three domestic servants at Craig-gowan and, adjacent, Rowanbank was constructed for Robert Gilroy's family. The Bughties was built for William Fergusson, owner of Dudhope Works, Douglas Street, Dundee. William Fergusson, a linen weaver from Hilltown, bought Dudhope Works in 1839 and established himself as a competitor to Baxter Brothers. Baxter Brothers, Princes Street, Dundee, were the worlds's biggest linen manufactures from about 1840 to 1890.

King Street, eastward, *c.* 1911. On the left behind the horse and cart stood the Free Masons Tavern. The bar once belonged to the owner of the local brewery, William Gray and Son, Fort Street. In1922 the tavern was taken over by Neil Smith, a former soldier in the Artillery at Broughty Castle and the name changed to the present Gunner's Bar. In 1846 William Gray moved from Dundee to take over a long established brewery in Fort Street. When the firm stopped brewing in 1923, they continued as bottlers and wine and spirit merchants.

King Street, eastward, 1913. The tobacconist and newsagents shop on the left would have been a source for local picture postcards and there is even a wall letterbox in which to post them. The advertisements on the side of the shop are for W.D. and H.O. Wills, Gold Flake; Three Castles and Capstan Navy Cut cigarettes and Lipton's Tea. A hanging sign advertises pies, bridies and pasties.

King Street, eastward, *c.* 1911. Local resident, David Grimmond has recorded being brought up in King Street around 1900. Aged about eight, David became a dedicated 'Amphibious Ancient' swimmer. From his attic bedroom window David was able to tell the time from the clock on the tower of the parish church. At 6.30am each summer morning, David turned up at Castle Green Pier to swim. David was taught to swim confidently in about three weeks by Mr Shaw, who had a boot shop in Brook Street.

7145 King Street, Broughty Ferry

King Street, eastward, *c.* 1936. On the left stands a solitary policeman in a street free of traffic. Gas lamps lighted King Street, and a fine example is seen on the right. One of BF's earliest portrait photographers, James Howie, had a studio at Cottage Place, King Street in 1867. James had moved to BF having spent the previous five years at a studio in Perth Road, Dundee. The BF studio closed after about a year.

Brook Street, Broughty Ferry

Brook Street, westward, 1906. The church on the left with a square tower was the West UF church, now demolished and replaced by flats. Beyond this is the spire of St Stephen's Established church with which the West church became united in 1963. The local newspaper the *BF Guide and Advertiser* was published every Friday by James Bedford and Co., printers and publishers, 246 Brook Street, for $\frac{1}{2}$ d.

Brook Street, westward, *c.* 1911. The building on the left with the clock was the Municipal Building with the police station just beyond. BF did not have a fire station at this time, but a hose was kept at the police yard in Long Lane. If there was a fire in BF, Captain James Jackson and five firemen would respond to a telephone call of 1212.

Brook Street, westward, *c.* 1912. The introduction of a half-holiday for shop assistants started in Dundee. In 1886 John and David Peebles opened their first grocery shop in Whitehall Street, Dundee. They gave their assistants a half-holiday every two weeks, within their first year of business. Together with other shopkeepers they established the weekly half-holiday. Dundee was the first large city to achieve this and after several years of effort, Winston Churchill, then MP for the city, brought in and carried the Shopkeepers' Half-Holiday Bill.

Brook Street, westward, *c.* 1926. A common sight in Brook Street or Gray Street around 1900 was a coachman with his carriage and a pair and long whip. The coachman would drive into Broughty to collect the messages or take his mistress around the shops. Another form of transport was a horse and phaeton, a light horse drawn four-wheeled carriage with or without a top. It was possible to hire such a vehicle for a Sunday morning or a day trip into the countryside.

Brook Street, westward, *c*. 1901. When the Shops Act of 1904 was introduced in BF there was a great deal of opposition from local traders who thought the reduced hours would damage their trade. The Act introduced shop closure from 2.00pm on Wednesdays, except over Christmas and New Year. Other exceptions were Wednesdays in weeks in which public holidays took place. When this picture was taken, the bank on the left had not been altered and Brook Street was still lit by gas lamps.

Brook Street, westward, *c*. 1903. The lighting in BF was originally supplied by the BF Gas Light Co. Ltd, formed in 1853. In 1870 the Burgh took over the gasworks and prices were steadily reduced over a period of a few years. In addition to gas lighting, electric lighting was installed in BF on 24 September 1902 under the BF Electric Lighting Order, 1900. An electric lamp is seen next to the bank on the left.

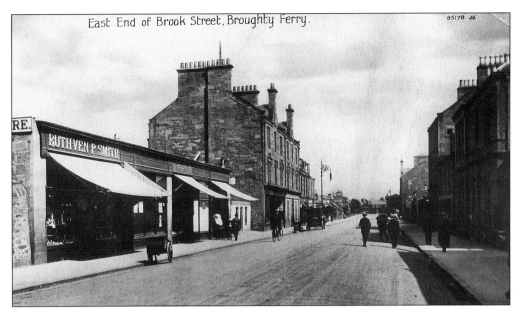

East End of Brook Street, Broughty Ferry.

85178 JV.

Brook Street, eastward, 1921. On 11 August 1902 the Electric Lighting Committee of BF Town Council met to discuss the number of electric street lights to be installed in BF. Councillor Gilles moved that twenty lamps should be installed and not just the twelve originally agreed upon. It was proposed that four lights should be placed in King Street, three more in Brook Street and one in Claypots Road. On a vote, six members voted for twelve lamps. The reason given for the lower number was one of expense.

East End of Brook Street, Broughty Ferry.

85179 JV.

Brook Street, eastward, 1921. On 24 September 1902 a ceremony took place in the Council Chambers inaugurating electric lighting in BF. Miss Lena Kidd, daughter of the electric light convenor, switched on the lights firstly in the Council Chambers and then afterwards the street lights. The building in which the electric plant was housed was situated at the northeast corner of the gasworks site, with a frontage in Brook Street. The gasworks can be seen on the right.

Brook Street, eastward, c. 1911. By September 1902 electric cables had been laid in Brook, Gray, Queen, Church, Fort, Grove and Castle Streets; Albert, Victoria, Strathern, Dundee, Ellieslie, Buchties and Camphill Roads; WF Bridge, Reres, Monifieth Roads and Abertay and Panmure Streets. In comparison, Dundee was one of the first cities in the country to establish a private supply of electricity. The original station was constructed on the site of the Old Cattle Market in Dudhope Crescent Road and public supply began in March 1893. In spite of this, gas street lights were still in use in Dundee in 1980. The old low bridge seen in the distance carried the pier branch line to the harbour station. The station and line closed in 1887.

Ramsay Park from east, c. 1908. The Ramsay family descended from Sir John Ramsay of Balmain. In 1806 Sir Alexander Ramsay of Balmain inherited family estates. In 1863 the site of Ramsay Park was acquired by Sir Alexander Ramsay. In 1875 Sir Alexander Ramsay, the forth baronet, received his title on his father's death. Sir Alexander Ramsay was born on 14 January 1837 and educated at Crewkerne and St Andrews. He died on 1st October 1902 at his residence, Owesden House, Lewes.

Ramsay Park, *c.* 1920. This is a quiet residential area. In days before private cars people lived closer to their place of work and used public transport. Today postcard publishers would not consider issuing postcards of side streets but during the Edwardian period most towns and cities were fairly comprehensively photographed.

Gladstone Terrace, *c.* 1920. Many commuters settled near the railway or tram route in newly built terraces and villas, where they enjoyed a good standard of living and were often able to employ a domestic servant.

Queen Street, westward, *c.* 1907. Tram car No.7 is on its way to Monifieth. East Queen Street UF church can be see on the left. This postcard was published by Davidson and Son, Kirkcaldy.

Monifieth Road, eastward, *c.* 1906. On the left is one of the twelve fine electric street lamps installed in 1902. The pillars of the street lights were designed by Walter MacFarlane and Co., Glasgow. In addition to the arc lamps each lamp pillar was fitted with two brackets for incandescent (16cp) lamps, which were lit after 12.00pm in place of the arc lamps. Similar lamps had been placed in the subway at BF Station in Gray Street.

Five
Buildings and Parks

Castleroy, Panmure Street, *c*. 1915. Two of the largest houses in BF were Castleroy, constructed by George Gilroy, and Carbet Castle, built by the Grimmonds. In 1891 George and Sarah Gilroy lived at Castleroy with their two sons, James K. and Alexander Bruce, and were supported by three housemaids, a cook, a kitchen maid, two table maids and an infirmary nurse. The estate was run and maintained by resident employees and their families. Those persons included a gardener at Castleroy East Lodge; a dairyman at 75 Panmure Street; two further gardeners and a groom at Castleroy Bothy; a coachman at the Coachman's House and a gatekeeper/joiner at the West Lodge. There was also a coachman and family at Gilroy Cottage, 65 Monifieth Road. After Sarah's death in 1909 the responsibility of Castleroy passed on to Alexander Bruce Gilroy, a managing director of Gilroy, Sons and Co. Ltd, Dundee. Many institutions benefited from Alexander Bruce's administrative ability and guidance. The positions he held included Director of Dundee Royal Infirmary; a governor of University College, Dundee; Chairman of Directors of the Royal Lunatic Asylum and of the Dundee branch of the RNLI. He was a trustee of Dundee Savings Bank for thirty years and became Deputy Chairman in 1900 and Chairman in 1917. In 1904 Alexander was appointed Director of the North British Railway. For relaxation he played golf and enjoyed curling. Alexander Bruce Gilroy, who never married, died on 14 November 1923, aged about 70 years.

Queen Street UF church, c. 1906. St Luke's Free church, not shown, was founded in July 1878 with a congregation of fouteen people. It was not until 12 January 1879 that the first minister, Revd William Wynne Peyton was appointed. For the first few years the congregation worshiped in the Iron church, a temporary corrugated iron building located to the west of the present church. On 27 November 1884 the new church was opened. St Luke's pioneered the use of a harmonium for church services. Introduced in the church in 1880, the harmonium was still used by the Sunday School in the late 1950s.

Queen Street UF church, c. 1909. In January 1953 the congregation of St Luke's and Queen Street church were united. St Luke's became the place of worship and Queen Street was transformed into halls. Queen Street church was founded in March 1873 with a congregation of fifty-three members. The first minister, Revd Andrew Carter, was appointed in November 1873 and the church building opened on 15 June 1876. In 1953 the joint congregation was almost 500 people. In 1969 Queen Street church halls were sold and today are used as a restaurant and snooker club.

St Mary's Episcopal church, Queen Street, *c.* 1904. St Mary's church was founded in 1848. Initially the congregation met in the school hall in Brook Street, which later became the site for the YMCA gymnasium. The building belonged to Thomas Erskine of Linlathern, one of the founders of the church. In 1858 the chancel and nave designed by Sir George Gilbert Scott were built. In 1870 the south aisle was added. Early congregations consisted of forty to fifty people. By 1910 the number had increased to 550.

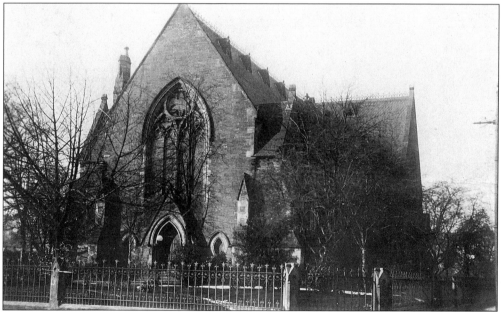

East UF church, Queen Street, *c.* 1908. In 1862 the West church was the only Free Church in BF. On 8 October 1862 the East Church Congregation was formed. Initially the congregation worshipped in Brook Street Hall owned by Thomas Erskine. The hall, on the site of the present YMCA gymnasium, burned down and the congregation worshipped in a temporary hall on the same site. The first minister, Revd Dr Murray Mitchell, was appointed on 10 September 1863 and by the end of the year the congregation had 145 members.

East UF church, *c.* 1907 Construction of the East church started in 1864 and on 21 December 1865 the church opened with a seating capacity for 600 people. In 1888 the harmonium was introduced and in January 1894 was replaced by the pipe organ. In 1900 the union of the Free Church of Scotland with the United Presbyterian Church occurred and the East Free church became the East United Free church. In 1929 the union of the Established Church and the United Free Church took place and the church became the East church of Scotland.

St Aidan's parish church, Brook Street, *c.* 1907. The parish church opened on 7 May 1826 to serve summer visitors and the expanding populations of East and West Ferry. St Aidan's was the first Established church in BF and was formerly constituted a chapel of Ease within the main parish of Monifieth in 1827. On 15 July 1863 the chapel was designated a parish church in its own right. For all non-church purposes the original parish with its boundaries remained the same.

St Aidan's parish church, *c.* 1906 Dr David Davidson, the first minister of the Established church, adhered to the Free Church in 1843. He signed the deed of demission on his deathbed on 22 August 1843. He thus became the first minister of the Free Church. An old bell bought by General Hunter of Burnside in 1772 was presented to the church by the General's son in 1827. The old bell had once hung on a pole at the Eagle Inn in King Street and was rung on festive occasions.

Westfield Road, *c.* 1906. The chapel on the right served the needs of Roman Catholics in BF. The spire on the left belongs to St Stephen's Established church. Just beyond St Stephen's, on the opposite side of the road, was the Western Public School. Other denominations were represented in BF. The Congregational Union church in Brook Street opened on 31 July 1864 and this was the first church in BF to use a pipe organ, which was installed in 1864. The Baptist church in St Vincent Street is still used as a place of worship.

St Stephen's church, Brook Street, *c.* 1909. St Stephen's was opened as a Chapel of Ease on 26 November 1871. The first minister, Revd Robert Scott, stayed for two years. In the late 1870s the church expanded with the construction of the chancel.

St Stephen's church, *c.* 1920. Early in 1963 the congregations of St Stephen's and the West church were united. St Stephen's became the place of worship and the West church, formerly a UF Church, was demolished and the land used to construct flats. The two school boys shown on the right were probably pupils of the Western Public School which was located opposite St Stephen's church.

HOME TERRACE, BROUGHTY FERRY

West UF church, Brook Street, *c.* 1911. At the Disruption of the Church of Scotland, in 1843, a minority of parish church members met to constitute a congregation of the newly formed Free Church of Scotland. The small Free Church congregation worshipped at first in a hall in Victoria Buildings in Gray Street. Despite their lack of numbers they raised sufficient funds to build the West church, shown on the left, within a few months.

West UF church and Hall, Church Street, *c.* 1903. The foundations of the West church were laid in September 1843. The first Free Church in the parish of Monifieth opened in March 1844 with Revd John Lyon, the first minister. A snowstorm prevented the arrival of invited preachers who should have spoken at the opening service, so Revd Lyon was left to open the church himself.

Eastern Public School, St Vincent Street, *c.* 1908. Around 1752 Dundee Kirk session managed a school in West Ferry. During the 1860s the school moved to Douglas Terrace, and later to larger premises in West Brook Street. The Sessional school was later acquired by the School Board and renamed the Western Public School. During the 1820s a hall in Brook Street was used as an infant school, supported by Thomas Erskine. In 1874 this building was given to BF YMCA (established 1866). In 1865 the Beach Mission built a school for the fishing community, which later became the Southern Public School, off Fisher Street. In 1910 the Southern had 460 pupils managed by one headmaster, one male and six female teachers.

Eastern Public School, St. Vincent Street, *c.* 1904. In the 1830s a hall in Gray Street was used as a school. In 1844 the Free Church erected a school in Fort Street. By 1870 this school was the largest in BF with about 200 pupils. With the formation of the School Board in 1873, Fort Street school was replaced by the Eastern school, built in 1874. By 1910 the Eastern had about 500 pupils, managed by William Sim, headmaster since 1874, and a staff of one male and nine female teachers.

Eastern School, Whinny Brae, *c.* 1926. The Eastern Primary School, Whinny Brae was built by BF School Board in 1911. Meanwhile the old school building was purchased by St Aidan's parish church and converted into halls. On 24 August 1964 Forthill Primary School, Fintry Place, opened with 235 boys and 213 girls following the closure of Grove Primary School, formerly the Western School. Forthill School was built on land acquired by Grove Academy as a recreation ground in December 1921. The Grove's playing fields were relocated to Dawson Park.

St Margaret's School, *c.* 1906. When the School Board was formed in 1873, BF had 1,076 school children. Of these 359(33%) attended private schools and 66(6%) were taught by private tutors and governesses. St Margaret's School, Viewbank, Hill Street, under the direction of Misses Kydd and Simpson, was one of four young ladies' seminaries in the area at this time. The others were Home Park School, Victoria Place, under headmistress Mrs Thomson and Gartlands school, Strathern Road under headmistress Miss Paterson; Bella Place School, East Brook Street, under headmistress Miss Shivess. Seafield House Preparatory School, 23 Seafield Road, was a private boys school managed by headmaster, Mr L.G. Wilkinson.

Grove Academy, Broughty Ferry

Grove Academy, Camperdown Street, *c.* 1907. The Education Act of 1872 introduced compulsory education in 1872 and an extension of the school learning age to 14 in 1883. This required the BF School Board to provide education for an increasing number of pupils at elementary level and beyond. This led to the development of Grove Academy. The Grove became a Board School on 10 September 1889 after taking over a school established in the 1880s in a house situated at the north east corner of the present site.

Grove Academy, *c.* 1911. The original house, called the 'Grove', had been a private school known as Mr Swan's Grove Seminary. In 1889 the school staff consisted of the headmaster, Mr A.H. Hutt, and two assistant teachers. When Mr Hutt was appointed in 1889, aged 24, the headship was his first job. His only previous experience was as a pupil teacher at his school in Fife and as a demonstrator whilst a student at Edinburgh University. Mr Hutt stayed at the Grove for almost 40 years until he retired in 1928.

Grove Academy, 1927. By 1889 the school was too small and the 130 pupils could not fit into the original house so extra space was found in the nearby Volunteer Hall, 51 Queen Street, which later became the Regal Cinema. In November 1890 the first phase of Grove Academy, to the west of the original house, was opened by the Earl of Strathmore. The pupil numbers continued to grow. By 1897 the original house had been demolished and a second wing built in its place. Until 1907 teachers taught all subjects. After 1907 specialist subjects were taught which required more staff.

Seafield House Preparatory School, 23 Seafield Road, c. 1908. Seafield House, seen from the cricket field, was a preparatory school for boys that closed in 1938. When the school leaving age increased to fifteen in the late 1930s, Grove Academy required more space. The site was acquired by the Grove for their extension building. Plans were made to lay the foundation stone in September 1939, but the Second World War intervened and the building was not opened until 1956. From the beginning Grove was a fee paying school from infants to advanced level. Infant and primary classes remained fee paying until well after the Second World War.

Municipal Building, Brook Street, *c.* 1908. In 1864 BF was incorporated as a Burgh and the Municipal Building was constructed shortly afterwards. The section with the wrought iron arch and clock was the Town Council offices and adjacent, beyond the clock, were the police offices. In 1989 the Council offices were extended at the rear to form a health and fitness centre while the rooms became available for public functions. The police station remains occupied and today a Safeway supermarket store is found just beyond.

THE BANK, BROUGHTY FERRY

North of Scotland Bank, 89 Gray Street, *c.* 1910. In 1910 BF had four banks. In addition to the North Bank, there was the Royal Bank of Scotland at 288 Brook Street; the Savings Bank at 74 Fort Street and the Post Office Savings Bank in Queen Street.

Lipton's grocery store, 68 Gray Street, 1937. Thomas Lipton was born in Glasgow on 10 May 1850 to parents who had left Northern Ireland the previous year to escape the potato famine. In 1860 Thomas left school and worked as an errand boy for a stationer. Aged 15, he had saved sufficient money from several small jobs to sail to New York where he progressed to working for a prosperous New York grocer. In 1869 he returned to Glasgow having gained experience in sales and advertising. In 1871 he opened his first grocer's shop in Stobcross Street, Glasgow. By the 1890s, through sheer hard work, the Lipton empire had been established with shops throughout Britain and trading contracts all over the world. In 1890 Lipton travelled to Ceylon and bought tea plantation land. It was the sale of cut price tea that made Lipton very wealthy. In 1895 Lipton was granted a Royal Warrant to supply tea to the Queen. Lipton never married but challenged five times for the America's Cup, as yachting was a great interest. Sir Thomas Lipton died on 2 October 1931 with no living relatives.

Confectioner, Donald Tolonetti's Refreshment Room, Castle Terrace, c. 1920. The café sold tea, coffee, ice cream and Fry's milk chocolate. The sale of ice cream was popularised by Italian street vendors and confectioners at the end of the nineteenth century. The ice cream block was first sold in Britain by Lyons in 1923.

Post Office, West Brook Street, *c*. 1906. Around 1802, letters to BF were kept at Dundee Post Office until they were called for or a carrier was employed to collect them. In 1829 a sub-post office was opened in BF which operated a penny postal service to and from Dundee. The BF office was managed by Peter Schleselman, a grocer at the corner of King Street and Fort Street. In 1906 Brook Street Post Office was open for business from 7am until 8pm weekdays and for one hour on Sunday mornings.

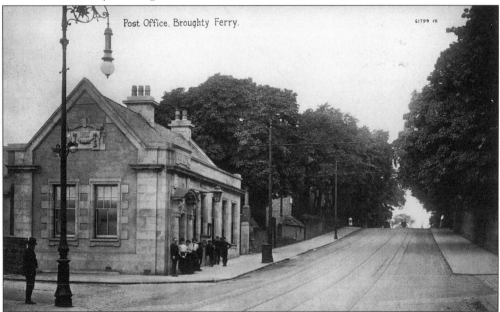

Post Office, Queen Street, 1908. Standing outside the new Post Office are a senior clerk, three counter girls wearing white blouses, and five postmen. All were waiting for Postmaster William Smeaton to open the door. On weekdays the post office was open for postal business from 7am to 8pm. On Sundays the office was open for postal and telegraph business from 9am to 10am. In 1908 there were nine mail collections from the post office on weekdays and one on Sunday. In BF in 1908 there were four mail deliveries during the week and three on Saturdays.

POST OFFICE, QUEEN ST., BROUGHTY FERRY.

Post Office, Queen Street, *c.* 1931. By 1931 the post office had been expanded by the addition of another floor. In 1931 the post office was open from 8am to 7.30pm on weekdays and from 9am until 10am on Sundays. There were now three mail deliveries a day, Monday to Friday, and two on Saturday. In 1931 there were eighteen wall letterboxes distributed between West Ferry and Barnhill, with six collections on weekdays, four collections on Saturdays and none on Sundays. Today the post office building is the Post Office Bar and restaurant.

Public Library, Queen Street, *c.* 1930. BF's first library, the Corbet Library, was instituted at the post office in Gray Street in 1864. When the post office changed location to Fort Street (*c.* 1876) and then to Brook Street (*c.* 1877), the library relocated. Around 1890 the Corbet Library was managed by the School Board. The site of the present library was donated by Ex-Provost Hunter of Dundee in 1922. The exterior was designed by J. McLellan Brown, Deputy Architect, Dundee, and opened on 24 October 1928. The library was extended in the 1970s.

Castleroy, c. 1925. Castleroy was designed for the jute manufacturer George Gilroy in 1867. It was the grandest mansion in BF, built in the Tudor style in 20 acres of ground. The house, reported to have almost 100 rooms and 365 windows, was occupied by George Gilroy's family. After the death of his two brothers, Robert on 20 October 1872 aged sixty-one years and Alexander in 1879; George Gilroy took over the management of Tay Works and brought his two sons into partnership. George Gilroy died on 12 January 1892 aged seventy-seven years and his widow Sarah Gilroy died on 17 March 1909 aged eighty-four years.

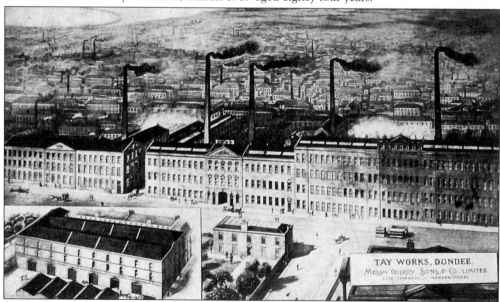

Tay Works, Lochee Road, Dundee, c. 1906. In 1836 William Boyack of Lochee Road was the largest flax spinner in Dundee, but in 1842 became bankrupt. In 1848 the Gilroys adopted jute instead of flax as a textile fibre. In 1849 Robert Gilroy, founder and senior partner of Gilroy Brothers, bought the Boyack Mills which had been unoccupied for seven years. The Gilroys substantially developed the site over the next thirty years. Tay Works became the world's second largest jute firm, with Cox Brothers Campendown Works, Lochee, as the biggest.

Castleroy, 1908. Tay Works was the first large purpose built jute mill and possibly the longest textile mill in Britain. The huge frontage was completed in Lochee Road in 1863 – 65. As one of the largest jute spinners and manufacturers in Dundee, Gilroy Brothers were able to make huge profits during the American Civil War (1861-65). Profits from this period led to the construction of Castleroy, which was designed shortly after the war. The Gilroys were one of the first Dundee manufacturers to establish direct importation of jute from India. They owned land near Calcutta for the cultivation of jute. For many years they owned their own ships, such as the *George Gilroy*, used in the 1860s to import jute.

Castleroy, c. 1926. In 1945 under the will of the late A.B. Gilroy, after termination of the last right of occupancy, Castleroy with grounds was offered to the Local Authority. After inspection of the site, Dundee Corporation turned the offer down as Castleroy had severe dry rot and it was financially unrealistic to convert the building into a hospital or convalescent home. In 1956 Castleroy was demolished. Today only the fine Tudor West Lodge in Hill Street survives. The grounds were not laid out as a public park but developed as sites for a few exclusive houses.

THE BLACK WATCH MEMORIAL HOME "DUNALISTAIR", BROUGHTY FERRY.

Dunalastair, 21 Hill Street, 1921. Dunalastair, constructed around 1827, was formerly named Fort House and occupied by General George Hunter in 1843. In 1866 the house was bought by Alexander Gilroy and remained in the Gilroy family until it was sold in 1920. Alexander Gilroy died on 18 July 1879.

BLACK WATCH WAR MEMORIAL HOME "DUNALISTAIR", BROUGHTY FERRY.

Dunalastair, Black Watch Memorial Home, 1921. On 9 February 1920 the building, including fittings and furnishings, were bought by the Black Watch for £11,047. Dunalastair was turned into a holiday home for families of soldiers lost in the First World War. In 1921 the first holidaymakers arrived and paid ten shillings a week to stay. A series of postcards of the house were issued in 1921 by Valentine and Sons Ltd, Dundee.

The lounge, Dunalastair, c. 1921. The lounge was the former billiard room, built around 1880 and was connected to the main house by a conservatory, now demolished. The photograph gives a fine impression of the splendour of the house. The reflection in the mirror shows the detail of the cornice and elaborate ceiling pattern. By the 1950s the ornate mirror above the fireplace had been replaced by a small solitary picture of a soldier but some of the same chairs were still in use with new covers. The lounge is now converted into flats, which have been named VC House.

IN THE GROUNDS AT DUNALISTAIR
(THE BLACK WATCH WAR MEMORIAL HOME), BROUGHTY FERRY

Grounds of Dunalastair, 1921. Dunalastair was situated in spacious grounds just to the West of Castleroy. There must have been fine views of BF from the observation tower in the centre of the picture. During the 1970s, as peoples' holiday expectations changed, Dunalastair's popularity began to decline. In 1984 Dunalastair was sold and the money raised was used to finance holidays of their choice for Black Watch families. After the sale the building was converted into self-contained flats.

Carbet Castle, 7 Camphill Road, *c.* 1915. Carbet Castle evolved from an earlier existing building, Kerbat House, which was probably built in the 1850s. Joseph Grimmond took up residence and renamed the property around 1860. The Castle was designed for the Grimmonds by Dundee architect T.S. Robertson and dates from 1866. Carbet Castle's interior decoration was lavish and several rooms had large marble fireplaces and elaborate painted ceilings. The fine ceilings, by French artist Charles Fréchou, were dated 1871. One such ceiling has been preserved and incorporated into the Mathew Building, School of Architecture in Perth Road, Dundee.

Carbet Castle, *c.* 1906. Joseph and Alexander Dick Grimmond, pioneers in jute carpeting, founded Bowbridge Works, Maxwelltown, Dens Road, Dundee. Construction of the works started in 1857 and the site expanded even further in the early 1870s and 1880s to become one of the largest works in Dundee. The works were demolished during the 1980s. In the late 1970s only part of the shell of Carbet Castle survived in a derelict state. In 1984 the last remaining section of the house was demolished. In August 1997 a new fifteen flat development incorporating towers and spires resembling the Castle was started.

Ballinard Hotel, *c*. 1940. Most of the large merchants' houses that survived demolition were turned into hotels or split into individual flats. The Ballinard was once the home of the Watson's whisky distillers. On 19 July 1906 one of the most destructive fires in Dundee took place at James Watson's bonded warehouse in the Seagate. The fire started shortly after 6pm when most of the staff had left. The warehouses contained nearly a million gallons of spirits, principally whisky and rum. The fire raged for two days before it was finally quelled. The aftermath of the fire was depicted on postcards at the time by Valentine and Sons Ltd.

Claypots Castle, West Ferry, *c*. 1904. Claypots Castle was built in 1569 and extended in 1588. The land was once attached to Lindores Abbey with the castle built at the time of the Reformation. Ownership of the castle passed from the Scrymgeours of Dudhope to John Graham of Claverhouse, Viscount Dundee and then to Archibald Douglas, the first Earl of Forfar. The building has been carefully restored as an ancient monument and is open to visitors.

Jubilee Arch, Reres Hill Park, *c.* 1905. Reres Hill Park has a sculptured archway, presented by James Guthrie Orchar, Provost of BF, to commemorate the Jubilee of Queen Victoria in 1887. J.G. Orchar, a wealthy businessman, was a partner in the firm of Robertson and Orchar, which manufactured machinery for the textile industry. After Queen Victoria died on 22 January 1901 the entrance to Reres was draped in purple and black for a period of mourning.

Reres Hill Park, *c.* 1906. In 1868 Reres Hill, a site of some $6\frac{1}{2}$ acres, was secured by the town commissioner for use as a public park from Lord Dalhousie. The cost of laying out walks and making other improvements to the land was met by the sale of wood from the necessary thinning of trees.

View from Reres Hill, westward, *c.* 1880. The two large mansions on the right, set in spacious grounds, with commanding views are Rosemount, with the large glasshouse, and Foxmount just beyond. Hidden in woodland behind these houses is Reres House, built in 1849. Reres House was the first of the large houses to be constructed. Others followed in the Hermitage, Camphill, and Mount Rosa areas. From 1858 Reres House was owned by James Soot, merchant, shipowner and insurance agent.

View from Reves Hill, eastward, *c.* 1906. Looking east from the top of Reres Hill a few large houses can be seen in spacious grounds. The large house, right of centre, in Tircarra, occupied at the time by Dundee merchant, George Newall Nairn. Mr and Mrs Nairn often travelled about town in a gleaming carriage, drawn by well-groomed horses and driven by an immaculate coachman in a top hat. Tircarra was one of the large houses, with grounds kept to perfection. The house has since been demolished to make way for a housing estate.

Orchar Park, 1913. The park is named after engineer, J.G. Orchar, born at Craigie, Dundee, in 1825. James completed an apprenticeship with his father as a joiner and wheelwright. He then was employed as an engineer at the old Wallace Foundry where he was involved in the construction of the first locomotives used on the Dundee and Perth Railway, opened in 1847. After a period working in England he returned to Dundee as a draughtsman at the Lilybank Foundry. In 1856 with William Robertson, a mechanic's shop manager at Baxter Brothers, he founded the Wallace Foundry which became world famous for the manufacturer of textile machinery.

Orchar Park, 1913. Robertson and Orchar Ltd specialised in the manufacture of machinery for spinning and weaving jute and linen. In 1886 James Orchar became Chief Magistrate of BF and was known there afterwards as 'Provost Orchar'. James retired from business in 1896 and on 14 May 1898 died, aged 73 years, at Angus Lodge, BF. Over the years Orchar had formed a fine collection of pictures and valuable violins which he bequeathed to the town. The violins, which included a Stradivarius, were sold by a nephew of Orchar to expand the collection of paintings. In 1913 there were three bowling clubs in BF.

Six

Transport

Paddle Steamer *Marchioness of Bute* on the Tay at Newburgh, *c.* 1913. In 1814 the steamboat the *Tay* was launched and she ran between Dundee and Perth. In 1822 the *Athol* was introduced on this route and in 1823 the *Tay* was replaced by the faster steamship the *Hero*. In 1846 it was possible to catch the daily steamboat *Royal Victoria* or *Lass O'Gownie* from Dundee to Newburgh or Perth. During the summer bathing season the two boats sailed to and from BF. The Dundee to Perth steamboat service declined and was later stopped for a time when the railway opened in 1847. Around 1913, paddle steamer trips up the Tay to Newburgh, Bridge of Earn or Perth were organised from Dundee. The two steamers which operated the route at this time were the *Carlisle* and the *Marchioness of Bute*. The *Carlisle* came to the Tay from the Thames in 1909 and sailed until requisitioned for war duties in 1915. The *Marchioness of Bute*, built in 1908, was formerly a steamer on the Clyde before arrival on the Tay in July 1980. The *Marchioness* was stationed at Portsmouth as a minesweeper during the war. After this she was kept at Inverkeithing and broken up in 1923.

BF from Forthill, c. 1914. From earliest times there was a river crossing at BF. The ferries remained in private hands until the nineteenth century. In 1818 there were five ferryboats which employed six boatmen. A few years later the Newport-Dundee crossing became more important and the Tayport-BF crossing became infrequent and unreliable. In 1846 the Edinburgh and Northern Railway Co. bought the river crossing to enable them to expand their route north. New harbours were built and a paddle steamer service introduced.

BF from the castle, c. 1905. The Pier Branch line is seen just behind the trawler. In 1848 the line was constructed from the end of the pier to BF where it connected with the Dundee and Arbroath railway for the journey to Dundee. The branch line was built by the Dundee and Arbroath Railway Co. (DAR) to delay the Edinburgh and Northern Railway Co. (ENR) from bridging the Tay. The rapid growth in railway construction in the 1840s led to strong competition between railway companies to control a direct route from London to Aberdeen.

BF from the castle, *c.* 1938. On the 31 May 1878, with the opening of the first Tay Railway Bridge, the Pier Branch line closed. However as a consequence of the Tay Bridge disaster, on the night of 28 December 1879, the Pier Branch line re-opened on 1 February 1880. On the same day the DAR and North British Railway Co. (NBR) came under joint ownership. Prior to the merger the NBR paid £9,000 a year to the DAR for the BF to Dundee rail link. When the new Tay Rail Bridge opened on 20 June 1887, the Pier Branch line was closed. The long hut seen on the end belonged to the Amphibious Ancients Bathing Association.

Ferryboat and castle, *c.* 1912. On 17 May 1848 the Edinburgh and Northern Railway Co., had completed the line to Tayport. Rail passengers boarded small paddle steamers such as *Auld Reekie* for the crossing from Tayport to BF. By 1862 the ENR had become incorporated in the North British Railway Co. The NBR operated larger freight carrying trains such as *Robert Napier*, which ran from Burntisland to BF. On one occasion the *Robert Napier* hit BF pier and seventeen wagons plunged into the Tay.

River Tay from BF, *c.* 1904. The paddle steamer *Dolphin* is shown arriving at BF from Tayport. The *Dolphin* left from the slipway on the west side of the pier. The first paddle steamer used for the Tay crossing was the *Mercury*. In 1845 the *Mercury* ran between Dundee, BF and Tayport, making five daily runs in each direction.

The *Dolphin* at BF pier, *c.* 1914. In 1890 a small paddle steamer the *Dolphin* was purchased for use by passengers only on the Tayport-BF crossing. Prior to this the *Dolphin* had been used in the construction of the Forth Railway bridge which opened in March 1890. By 1920 the *Dolphin* ferry service had become uneconomic to operate and she was replaced. Tayport was formerly known as Ferryport-on-Craig until the name was changed by the Edinburgh and Northern Railway Co.

Harbour, *c.* 1905. These five schoolboys were probably waiting for the ferryboat to take them to Tayport. As there were no secondary schools on the Fife side of the Tay, school children had to cross the Tay from Tayport to BF and from Newport to Dundee until the early 1930s. The distance from Tayport to BF is about a mile, and the distance from Newport to Dundee about two miles. On some days the crossing could be quite rough and on others the river could become shrouded in mist.

TAYPORT BOAT AT BROUGHTY FERRY.

Motor Ferry boat, *c.* 1931. The *Dolphin* was replaced by the motor launch *Abertay* shown here. The motor ferryboat, which used the Fisherman's Pier, was really quite small. There was some shelter inside and open wooden benches for passengers outside. The crossing to Tayport took ten minutes and six double journeys were made daily. The service started from Tayport at 8.30am and the last departure from BF was at 5pm. The *Abertay* was withdrawn from service in 1939 and not replaced, ending this crossing.

Entrance to BF railway station, Gray Street, *c.* 1904. At the end of the line of shops is the entrance to BF station, behind which is the high signal box. Two milkmen with carts delivering milk from churns have stopped at the closed railway gates. It was not until the late 1920s that milk was delivered in glass milk bottles. In the background, Carbet Castle, the home of the Grimmonds, can be seen. The railway made BF accessible to the people of Dundee for recreation and for the better off, gave access to a quiet suburb in which to live.

BF Station, Gray Street, *c.* 1905. The Dundee and Arbroath Railway, which passed through BF station, opened on 6 October 1838. There was a temporary terminus at Craigie, well to the east of Dundee. The first train, which departed Craigie at noon, consisted of eleven coaches and carried 400 passengers. On the return journey from Arbroath, an average speed of 26 mph was achieved. Horse buses provided the connections to and from Dundee. The first six engines used on this line were built in Dundee by Kinmond, Hutton and Steel.

BF Station, 1925. BF station was one of the original Dundee and Arbroath Railway stations, dating from 1838. However, on 21 July 1879 the North British Railway was granted joint ownership of the Dundee to Arbroath section. Most of the station was rebuilt during the period of joint ownership, probably around the turn of the century. A train timetable of 1847 states that the adult single fares from Dundee to BF were 6d, 4d and 3d for first, second and third class respectively.

High signal box, BF station, c. 1912. Around 1910 a yearly season ticket on the railway between Dundee and BF cost £3; Dundee to Barnhill cost £3 10s. Many commuters caught the 1.10pm train at East Station to return to BF for lunch and the 6.10pm train home in the evening. If you travelled home for lunch this totalled twenty two journeys a week, which came to 1s 2d or 1s 4d for the week which was less than one penny a journey. The original mechanism for the level crossing gates was installed in 1887 and was upgraded in the 1920s. The gates remained until recently as the only working pair left of this design in Scotland.

West Ferry Station, 1906. By 1840 the Dundee and Arbroath Railway terminated at Trades Lane station near the docks in Dundee. Trades Lane terminus was adjacent to the northside of Victoria Dock and consisted of a simple long wooden shed, 320 feet by 30 feet, without a waiting room. This station was replaced by Dundee East Station, which opened on 14 December 1851. Eight years later West Ferry station was opened.

West Ferry Station, 1913. West Ferry Station was opened by the Dundee and Arbroath Railway in 1859 and served a growing residential area. The station survived until 4 September 1967 when passenger services were withdrawn. On the same day Easthaven and Elliot Junction stations, also on the Dundee to Arbroath line, closed to passengers. Today only the West Ferry Station building survives as a partially occupied residence.

West Ferry Station, *c.* 1903. The previous two pictures of West Ferry Station were taken by Valentine and Sons Ltd, Dundee. It was quite usual for an early image printed in black and white to be updated after a few years and to be printed in a different style. The real photograph image shown above is by G.W. Wilson and Co., Aberdeen.

Barnhill Station, *c.* 1931. Barnhill was the first station on the rural branch line from BF to Forfar, which opened on 14 September 1871. Passenger numbers were never high although at one time Barnhill was the busiest place on the line. The station closed on 10 January 1955 when passenger services from BF to Forfar ceased. Barnhill operated as a goods station until closure on 9 October 1967, by which time the station building and platforms were derelict. The station site has now been built over.

Opening Day – Dundee and BF and District Tramways Co. Ltd route, at the original Union Street terminus, Monifieth, 27 November 1905. At 11am on the opening day, three decorated tramcars left Dundee High Street loaded with guests. When Craigie Terrace, the Burgh boundary was reached, the first car broke through a coloured ribbon stretched across the lines. The Ex-Provost Brownlee of Dundee, the company chairman, then gave a short speech from the top of the first car. The cavalcade then passed through decorated streets of BF to Monifieth. The party then returned to Dundee for a formal lunch. Ex-Provost Brownlee is standing to the left of the tramcar.

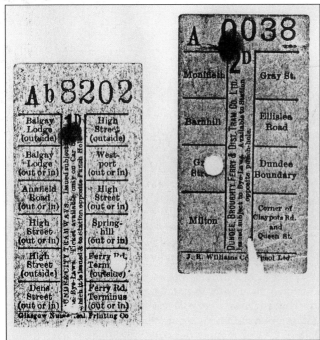

Tramway tickets, 27 December 1905. The public were allowed to use the tram service at 2pm and many interested passengers explored the line. The tickets shown here were issued to a traveller on the opening day. The fare from Dundee High Street to the boundary was 1d(outside). At the boundary the Dundee Corporation driver and ticket collector got off and the company crew took over. The fare from the Dundee boundary to Gray Street, BF, was 2d. The buff coloured 1d ticket (left) is punched in the position of Ferry Road terminus (outside). The purple coloured 2d ticket is punched in the position of Gray Street and has the low-ticket No. 0038.

BF tramcar No.5, 1929. The system of changing crews at the boundary was soon found to be inconvenient. From February 1906 a single crew was employed for the complete route. Before the First World War a service of ten-minute frequency was provided. The tram provided a popular and cheaper means of commuting than the train. During the war period track maintenance was poor. In 1931 Dundee Corporation took over the Tramway Company and decided to close the line.

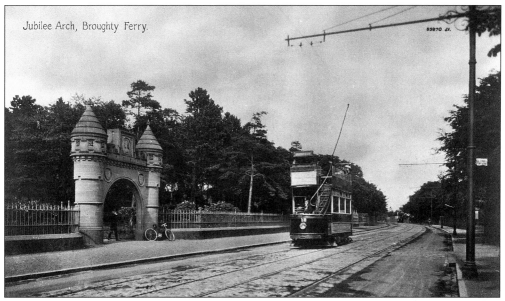

Jubilee Arch, Monifieth Road, 1906. Tramcar No.12 is on its way to Monifieth with the conductor standing at the rear watching the photographer. On the right, attached to the overhead wire support pole is a tramway stop sign stating 'All cars stop here'. In 1887 the nearby Orchar Park, a site of about $6\frac{1}{2}$ acres, was named to honour Provost Orchar. The land was acquired by the town commissioners but the wall and railings were a gift from James Orchar.

Taxi rank outside BF Station, 1906. Around 1900 a traveller wishing to visit Newtyle or Coupar Angus would take the train to Dundee East Station. On arrival a horse-drawn bus would take passengers along Dock Street to Dundee West Station. A train would then take passengers via Ninewells Junction and Lochee to Coupar Angus. Generally, if you did not arrive in time to catch your train it was customary for the head porter to close the station gate preventing access to the platform and you would have to wait for the next train.

Gray Street, c. 1926. In 1826 a return coach service operated three times a day from Dundee post office to the Eagle Inn, King Street, BF. Parked outside the station is a charabanc with a canvas roof. Between 1905 and 1915 charabancs had a fold-back hood, side doors enabling access to tiered seats and solid rubber types. Between 1915 and 1925 the design was similar but the seating was all on the same level. Between 1925 and 1930 the fold-back hood had incorporated side screens and vehicles had pneumatic tyres. By 1930 the vehicle had evolved into the fully enclosed single decker coach.

Seven
Events

THE AUSTRALIAN LINER "ULIMAROA" ASHORE AT WEST FERRY BEACH. DEC. 1907.

The Australian Liner, *Ultimaroa*, ashore at West Ferry beach, 2 December 1907. The 450 passenger liner *Ultimaroa* had been launched from Gourlay Brothers' Camperdown shipyard, Dundee in July 1907. The ship was approaching completion and whilst undergoing steaming tests ran aground on the afternoon of 2 December. Efforts to remove the 5,700 ton, 400 foot long vessel against the tide failed and during the evening she developed a list to port. Two tugboats *Gilroy* and *Renown* accompanied by two local trawlers, freed the vessel at the afternoon tide on 3 December and the two tugboats pulled the ship back to Dundee. No serious damage was expected because of the soft sand. However Dundee and Leith docks were too small to inspect such a large vessel so she was transported to the Tyne for a survey and repair. The Valentine and Sons photographer, perhaps a resident of BF, was very alert to capture this fine news picture.

Tay Bridge Disaster, 1879. The first Tay Bridge, shown above after the disaster, was designed by Thomas Bouch (1822-1880). It took six years to complete and was opened on 31 May 1878. In June 1879, Queen Victoria crossed the bridge and conferred a knighthood on Bouch. On the night 28 December 1879, a great storm struck the bridge just as the passenger train was crossing. The central high girders section of the bridge collapsed and the train plunged into the Tay at the cost of about 75 lives.

A section of the first Tay Bridge, BF beach, 1 April 1880. The 245 foot bridge span containing four carriages, engine and tender was cut into sections using dynamite. The section containing the carriages was raised on 1 April and brought to BF beach where it was photographed with the carriage still inside it. The water pipe, shown bottom right, brought the water supply from Dundee to Newport. On 6 April 1880 the girder section containing the guard's van and a second class carriage was raised and towed to BF.

96

The Engine, Old Tay Bridge Disaster

NBR No.224 engine, Dundee, April 1880. On 7 April 1880 the engine was raised from the Tay using pontoons and lifting chains. The engine sank twice before successfully reaching Tayport on 11 April. Unfortunately the engine cab was damaged by an anchor cable from a recovery vessel. The engine and tender were taken to Dundee where they were photographed by Valentine and Co.

Old Tay Bridge Disaster. The Tender.

NBR No.224 tender, Dundee, April 1880. From the day NBR No.224 was lifted from the Tay she became known as the *Diver*. After the accident the engine was repaired in Glasgow. She was rebuilt in 1885 and again in 1897. In 1919 she was withdrawn from service after a working life of 48 years. The second Tay Bridge was designed by Sir William Arrol (1839-1913). Fourteen men lost their lives over the five-year construction period. The new bridge opened for passenger traffic on 20 June 1887.

Lord Roberts' visit to Broughty Castle, 19 August 1903. Lord Roberts', Commander-in-Chief of the British Army, visited Dundee with the object of inspecting Tay defences at BF. He arrived by train in the afternoon and was greeted by crowds of people. He was then taken by carriage along Gray Street and King Street to the castle where he spent thirty minutes inside. The photograph was taken by John A. Rodger, probably from his photographic studio window at 266 Brook Street.

Lord Roberts' visit to Broughty Castle, 19 August 1903. On leaving the castle Lord Roberts embarked the mine-laying steam launch the *General Stothart*. After inspecting the defence minefields he arrived in Dundee where an awaiting carriage took him to the Queen's Hotel. In the evening he presented prizes to the Dundee Highlanders in the Drill Hall. During the event Lord Roberts was made Honorary Colonel of the regiment. After an overnight stay at the Queen's Hotel, Lord Roberts returned south.

The Lord Mayor's coach at the corner of Fintry Place and Seafield Road, 30 July 1904. Sir James Thomson Ritchie, born in Dundee in 1835 and educated at Dundee High School, became Lord Mayor of London in 1903. In 1904 he had the Lord Mayor's state coach plus four drays shipped to Dundee. On 30 July the Lord Mayor travelled from Airlie Park, BF, the residence of host Lord Provost Barrie, to the Town House, Dundee. Thereafter a procession of sixteen carriages made a six mile tour of Dundee before Sir James was awarded the freedom of the city in a ceremony at the Kinnaird Hall.

Parade in Camp, Castle Green, c. 1904. The Tay Division of Submarine Miners Royal Engineers (Volunteers) was founded on 17 March 1888 and based at BF castle. Their aim was to assist in the deployment of underwater mines to protect commercial ports. As part of their training all Volunteer units held an annual camp close to their base. In November 1907 the War Office withdrew underwater mines for British ports and the Tay Division Volunteers were disbanded.

Parade of Tay Division Volunteers, Gray Street, *c.* 1905. Most Volunteers were amateur part-time soldiers who participated in their free time. The soldiers used to camp for two weeks every summer on Castle Green. On Sundays they marched up St Vincent Street to church. On the last day of the camp they put on a show at the pier. The parade here is perhaps a prelude to publicise the show.

BF Station, Boys Brigade leaving for camp, 25 July 1903. Eighty-five members of the First BF Company of the Boys Brigade set off on the Saturday morning for a week's camp at Edzell. The group was led by Captain George H. Coutts and seconded by Lieutenant Robert J. Lindsay. On the Sunday they marched to the Established church in Edzell for a special service in which the band participated.

BF Boys Brigade Bazaar, YMCA Gymnasium, 27-28 November 1903. Members of the Boys Brigade are wearing bandages and displaying a wood and canvas stretcher. Gesturing, two of the boys have taken off their caps to collect money. The aim of the two-day sale of work was to raise money for an American organ for the Brigade Bible Class and to provide additional funds for other musical instruments. The gymnasium had been attractively decorated for the occasion. The Reading Room 'transmogrified with flowers and plants' proved very popular. At the end of the day one, over £268 had been raised. A further £162 was raised on the Saturday. Many of BF's society ladies attended the event. They included Mrs Don, The Lodge; Mrs MacKenzie, Harecraig; Mrs Stephen, Helensea; Miss Gibson, Invertay; Mrs Guthrie, Hope Park; Mrs Gilroy, Castleroy and Mrs Ogilvy from Airlie Lodge.

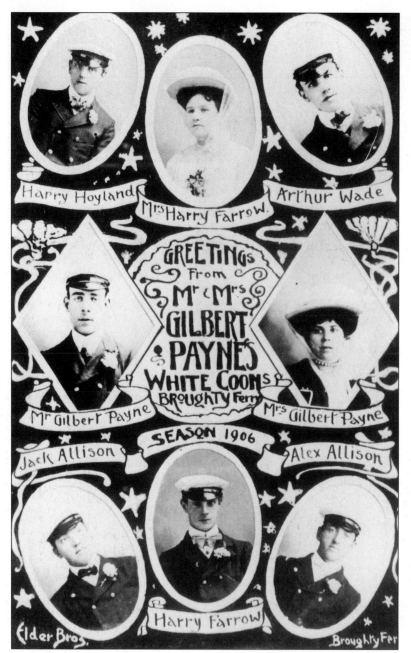

Mr and Mrs Gilbert Payne's White Coons, 1906 season. In Victorian times minstrel shows became a feature of the seaside holiday. Gradually groups of entertainers took over from individual performers. The first minstrel troupe, the Virginian Minstrels, visited Britain from America in 1843. They were very popular with their black make up, bright blazers and melodic plantation songs. By the 1860s most large seaside resorts had their own white minstrels with blackened faces. By the late 1890s the minstrels had been replaced by pierrots. Pierotts first appeared in England in 1891. The all-male troupers gradually included women in their performances. Old postcards provide a useful record of BF's entertainers who performed initially on a makeshift stage on the beach and later in the grounds of Orchar Park.

The White Coons, 1906 season. The White Coons stage clothes were nautical-style outfits for the men and evening gowns for women. At the time there was a genuine thrill to hear Mrs Payne sing, especially in the evening with the moon on the Tay and the water lapping softly on the shore. Some of the songs performed were evangelical and included *Father in Heaven Above* and *Holy City*. The message on the back of the postcard reads 'I was through seeing my sister in the Ferry so I went down to the sands and heard these people singing. I enjoyed it very much.'

Leslie Lynn's Entertainers, 1911. Different troupes performed on the beach in different summer seasons. Generally if performers made a name for themselves they would move on. Many famous stage and music hall stars started their careers as beach performers in seaside towns. If a performance received a good review, couples from the large houses turned up in full evening dress as if they were attending Her Majesty's Theatre in Dundee.

The Sands, 1913. A crowd has gathered around a makeshift stage on the beach. The entertainers were the Bachelor Boys using a small stage without wings or scenery. Although the weather is fine, people are well dressed up in warm clothes and hats. It was normal for visitors to wear hats at the seaside at this time, even on hot summer days.

The Bachelor Boys, *c.* 1914. By this time the Bachelor Boys comprised of eight men dressed in white sailors' outfits. Compared to the 1913 season (above) they had enlarged their stage on the beach. In the centre an upright piano can be seen but generally the stage looks quite bare. Performances were held at 3pm and at 7.45 pm, daily. Seats to view the show cost 2d but many people watched from a distance for nothing!

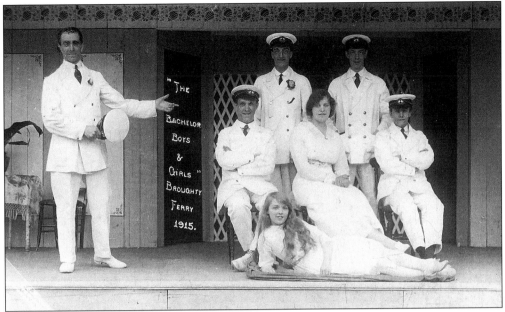

The Bachelor Boys and Girls, 1915. By 1915 the Bachelor Boys had been reduced to five men but two girls had been introduced. The performances were now held in Orchar Park instead of on the Sands. The seaside entertainers sometimes performed outdoors in Dundee. Certainly in 1905 entertainers performed on a small make-shift stage on Magdalene Green, sited between the Bowling Green and Esplanade Station.

The Bachelor Boys and Girls, 1915. The stage looks more attractive than it did in 1915. The piano has been moved off centre to the right and a large plant and hanging baskets have been introduced. The girls may have had some influence in this or perhaps the park keeper helped. Performances were held daily at 3pm and 7.30pm. The new location enabled six overhead stage lights to be introduced for the evening shows. Charlie Newcomb is on the left with Vi next to him. Bobbie Burns is on the right.

THE GRAND *Theatre de Luxe.*

West King Street, Broughty Ferry.

'The Black Box,'

Successor to THE MASTER KEY.

Universal Special Feature Serial in Fifteen Weekly Episodes.

(Each Two Parts.)

Story by E. Philips Oppenheim, the Great English Author.

What does it Contain?

Read it in " The Bro'ty Advertiser."

An Advertisement for the Grand Theatre de Luxe, West King Street, 1915. The Grand Theatre de Luxe used postcards to promote their new serial *The Black Box* by E. Philips Oppenheim. The film was serialised in fifteen weekly parts by the Trans-Atlantic Film Co. Ltd, and starred actress Anna Little. The Grand Theatre closed in 1939. The *Broughty Ferry Advertiser* was painted and published by James Belford and Co, Brook Street every Friday and sold for ½ d.

The BF Picture House, 1933. The Picture House opened in 1918. In 1952 the name was changed to Reres Cinema. Reres Cinema showed continuous performances from 6.15 pm, alternating A and B films. The audience could walk in at any point during the shows and often in the middle of a film. Reres Cinema closed in 1963. Other cinemas in BF included the Universal Cinema, Laurence Street (1914-1915); the Capitol Cinema, 95 Church Street (1936) and the Regal Cinema, Queen Street (1937-60).

The Great Annual Sale at J.R. Bell's, *c.* 1909. Several local firms used postcards successfully to promote their businesses.

Open Air Singing at Broughty Ferry.

Open air singing, on the beach, *c.* 1910. Regular concerts were held in Reres Park, Orchar Park and on the Esplanade where a bandstand had been erected in 1894. In 1910 the first Sunday concert was held on BF sands and money was raised for the lifeboat appeal. The singing event shown here is a more informal fringe activity.

Ye Amphibious Ancients (YAA), BF pier, c. 1907. The 'Ancients' founded in 1884 had their headquarters at the Castle harbour where they extended their welcome to visitors of both sexes. During the summer months members would meet for a dip at 6.30am to 8.30pm weekdays; 8am to 9.30am Sundays and at 7pm Mondays to Fridays. Bathing was prohibited when a ferry steamer was at the pier with passengers landing or boarding, or outside Association hours. On New Years Day the YAA held a gala. The YAA Bathing Association remains as the only open water swimming club in Scotland and still offers a hectic summer program of events.

Ye Amphibious Ancients, c. 1910. The YAA taught swimming free all the year round. The season recommended for invalids or those in delicate health was from 1 April until November. For enthusiasts there were great challenges. On 19 August 1911 two sixteen-year-old girls swam from BF pier to Tayport. Several spectators gathered to watch Frances Suttie and Bella Burnett plunge into the fast flowing Tay for their long swim. Several male swimmers were in the water in front and behind them. The timekeeper recorded that Miss Suttie took 50 minutes to complete the one mile crossing with Miss Burnett just $1\frac{1}{2}$ minutes behind.

Ye Amphibious Ancients, *c.* 1912. Mr Alex Millar, a banker, was the only man to complete the crossing on 19 August 1911. A well known lady swimmer swam the distance some years ago but this was a first time achievement for teenagers. There was keen competition between local swimming clubs. On the same day Mr H. Groocock of Newport Swimming Association attempted to swim from Newport to Dundee and back.

YE AMPHIBIOUS ANCIENTS 1925.

Ye Amphibitious Ancients, 1925. Mr Groocock set off from Newport at 2.15pm and aimed for Dundee baths but the strong down current took him to the jetty, which he touched at 3.10pm. Without a rest he turned around and swam back but exhausted had to climb into a rescue escort boat on the Newport side of the *Vulcan* within a few yards from the shore. He later recovered from exhaustion and was able to walk home, with assistance. Mr Groocock was disappointed as he had already completed the swim from Newport to Dundee in 1909.

A horse and cart studio photograph, *c.* 1906. This cabinet photograph is by Philip E. Low whose main studio was in Bath Street, Portobello. In the summer Mr Low set up temporary studios on the Promenade, BF, at the Bathing Station, Aberdeen and at 130 Leith Street, Edinburgh. The lady holding the child is believed to be Mrs Jackson of 22 Barrack Street, Perth. The painted backdrop is of the High Street, Dundee, with the Townhouse on the night. The photographer has recorded this image as number 915.

Rowing boat, studio photograph, *c.* 1911. A visiting family has posed against a painted backdrop of Broughty Castle. Father is in a dark lounge suit, mother wears a dark jacket, the son has a dark sailor jacket and the youngest two are dressed in white. All the family are wearing hats; everybody wore hats at the seaside and on the beach until just before the First World War. The photographer was probably Mr D.G. Brown.

Early motor car, studio photograph, *c.* 1911. The photograph by D.G. Brown shows five smartly dressed children grouped around a painted wooden car. Two of the younger girls are wearing dark blue sailor outfits and broad brimmed straw hats. Queen Victoria started the fashion for sailor suits when she dressed her sons in sailor outfits in the late 1850s. From the 1860s until the 1920s, sailor suits were standard summer wear for boys of all classes. Girls also dressed in this style but wore skirts. Over the period from 1900 to 1920, boys sailor suits were more often white, rather than the dark blue of the 1890s.

Motor car, studio photograph, *c.* 1914. The small wooden motor car (above) was replaced by a real car. The same Dundee backdrop has been used by a photographer, Mr Brown. The gentleman driver is wearing a suit with waistcoat, collar and tie and straw boater. In the 1870s the straw boater had been adopted for boating. By the 1890s the boater had become high fashion. The sides of the hats were decorated with plain or striped ribbon. At this time holiday visitors did not seeka suntan, and women always wore a hat and sometimes carried a parasol.

Motor car, studio photograph, *c.* 1914. This photograph is by Mr D.G. Brown, resident photographer at the Promenade for the summer seasons from around 1911 to 1915. Similar photographs exist, probably taken in Edinburgh, with a painted backdrop of Princess Street looking towards Carlton Hill, with the Royal Academy on the right. During the 1880s women wore tailored suits. On warm days women would take their jackets off but men always wore their blazers.

Motor car, studio photograph, *c.* 1914. Three young men, perhaps brothers, are very smartly dressed in suits, collars and ties and straw boater hats. The photograph is again by D.G. Brown and recorded as image number 394.

Eight

Barnhill

Dalhousie Road, westward, 1905. Barnhill was a village which became an eastern suburb to BF as the two areas developed. The Dundee to Monifieth tram route ran through Barnhill, which encouraged further housing development close to the line. Tramcar No.9 is seen on its way to Monifieth. In front of the houses on the left, kerbstones have been laid to mark the edge of the levelled earth pavement. Where there are gaps between houses, the edge of the road has been left as a natural grass footpath.

The Sands, Barnhill, *c*. 1931. The clean sandy beach was well patronised by local inhabitants. By today's standards the boys are dressed in poorly fitting jumpers and jackets. They show no interest in the photographer as cameras had become more compact and common place by the 1930s. The photograph was taken by Thomas S. White of J.B.White Ltd, Cowgate, Dundee. In the 1930s Thomas White started using a 127mm Exacta camera and around 1943 bought a compact 35mm Leica camera.

The Beach, Barnhill, *c*. 1932. The popularity of Barnhill beach is seen at the height of summer. The two wooden framed sets of swings were used by both boys and girls. This is one of a series of twenty-five sepia-tinted photographic postcards of Barnhill published by J.B. White Ltd, in the 1920s and 1930s.

Clubhouse, Barnhill Links, West End, *c.* 1915. BF Ladies Golf Club was established at Barnhill in 1895. The Clubhouse, shown on the left, was built out of ornamental timber with a weather board exterior. The roof was constructed with painted, Canadian pattern galvanised steel. Barnhill links was a short nine-hole course for ladies and beginners. In 1895 the annual subscription was five shillings. In 1939 a round of golf cost 2d (1p) a round. Barnhill Links was a busy course so people often had to queue to play. A full time green keeper was employed.

THE PROMENADE, BARNHILL.

Promenade, Barnhill, *c.* 1915. Four lady golfers have gathered for the photographer. Seasoned golfers could play at BF Golf Club at Monifieth or travel to Carnoustie. BF Golf Club was established in 1878. Alexander Bowman was the first club secretary until 1889 when he became club captain. Around 1910 the Haskell rubber-cored golf ball was launched in Britain amidst a great deal of controversy. Once you had played with a rubber-cored ball it was unbearable to play with an old 'gutty', which was like hitting a stone.

Collingwood Terrace, *c.* 1910. In front of the row of terraced houses, space has been levelled as an unmade road. The gaslight in this, and a few of the other pictures from this period, show no lantern.

Barnhill from Links, 1905. Cows from a local farm sometimes invaded the village. They came down to graze but often got out of hand and wandered into peoples' gardens. The cattleman would do his best to keep them under control. In the summer the wide open spaces in the village were a blaze of golden gorse and broom.

Invermark Terrace, 1905. Four people and a dog have stopped to watch the photographer with his large wooden camera and tripod. This is one of a small cluster of photographers of Barnhill taken by Valentine and Sons Ltd, Dundee in this year.

Kerrington Crescent, 1905. Forthill Athletic Football Club played on a football ground situated behind Kerrington Crescent. Crowds of over 1,000 were sometimes present. One year a league decider match against Dundee Violet attracted over 2,000 spectators who saw Forthill win 6-4.

Kerrington Crescent, c. 1915 The street has expanded since the previous earlier photograph was taken in 1905. The sender of the postcard has marked the card with a small cross to indicate her home. The postcard was published by stationer, Robert Lundie, Dundee.

The Milton, near Barnhill, c. 1915. Three boys on the riverbank of Dighty Burn and a gardener with a long white beard have spotted the photographer and watched his activities. The postcard was published by Robert Lundie, the stationer in Reform Street, Dundee. The message on the postcard says 'This is a view of Lizzie's house, back of it. You will see from it that she can spend all day out of doors'.

The 'Wylde', 13 Panmure Terrace, *c.* 1933. The 'Wylde' at one time belonged to William Watson, owner of Forebank Dye works, Victoria Road, Dundee. The firm specialised in dying, bleaching and finishing all kinds of flax, cotton and jute yarns. Around 1933 the 'Wylde' became Shepherds Convalescent Home before being turned into Woodlands hotel some twelve years later. Today the hotel boasts a new extension, replacing the hedge in front of the house. New facilities include a conference centre and swimming pool. Each of the seventeen individually designed guest rooms in the main house now possesses en-suite facilities.

Miller's Dam, *c.* 1930. The Mill Dam, centre left, was a part of Balmossie Mill. The mill Lade, which served the Bleachfields at Milton, was filled in during 1947. The old grain mill contained some carved stones probably derived from the nearby site of the chapel of Eglismonichty.

Dalhousie Road, eastward, *c.* 1915. The building on the right was the original Barnhill Post Office which is seen again on the left in the westward view of Dalhousie Road. Barnhill Post Office opened as a town sub office on 3 January 1911. Tramcar No.33 is seen on the left on an empty road.

Dalhousie Road, eastward, 1949. Barnhill Post Office can be seen on the right with a standard red K6 telephone kiosk, designed by Sir George Gilbert Scott in 1935. The tramlines, overhead wires and support poles have been removed but the gas street lights remained.

Dalhousie Road, westward, *c*. 1911. Tramcar No.6, en route for Monfieth, is stationary at the tram stop. The conductor has walked to the front of the tram to watch the photographer. This stretch of track had single rails but just beyond the railway bridge the line was double track. The railway bridge, now removed, carried the Dundee and Forfar branch railway. There are cobbles in the centre of the road holding the tramlines in place. Either side water has collected in the potholes of the earth road surface and in the gutter of the cambered road. The pavement is made of earth, edged with kerbstones.

Dalhousie Road, westward, *c*. 1930. A covered tram is on the Dundee to Monifieth route. For many years the trams were open-topped and the driver stood unprotected from the weather. The long, bumpy, uncomfortable journey took three-quarters of an hour. In midwinter the journey seemed an eternity for passengers who had to sit in the rain or sleet in an open top deck when the inside was full. The last trams ran in this route on 15 May 1931. When the trams were scrapped they were replaced by Leyland double-decker buses.

St Margaret's church, *c.* 1932. St. Margaret's church began as a chapel of Ease of the parish church of Monifieth. The first service was held on 8 June 1884 in a corrugated iron building acquired from St Luke's, BF. The Tin Kirk, as it was known, was used until 1895. The nave of the new church was dedicated on St Margaret's Day, 16 November 1895. The first minister, Revd Thomas N. Adamson, was ordained on 30 October 1884 and remained the minister for twenty seven years. In March 1907, St Margaret's became a parish church in its own right. The Tin Kirk building is still in use as a church hall.

Cottage Orphanage, 6 Abercrombie Street, *c.* 1915. Barnhill Orphanage was founded in 1886 by Revd Thomas N. Adamson, minister of St Margaret's parish church. The cost of the construction of the orphanage was £300, of which £200 was lent to the trustees by Revd Adamson's mother and £100 was borrowed from the North of Scotland Bank in BF. Six or seven children were brought up at a time. Finance for their upbringing was made partly from family money and partly from members and friends of the church. Since, the Cottage Home has served as the church officer's house for many years.

Housing, 6 Abercrombie Street, c. 1911. The building shown is situated directly across the road from what was the Cottage Orphanage. The postcard was sent on 21 September 1911 by a lady visiting the area. The message on the back of the card reads 'We went on a steamer to Perth last Tuesday. We started from Dundee at 10.15am. The journey takes two hours there, with two hours to look around and have dinner. We arrived back at 4.00pm. The scenery was lovely.'

Barnhill Cemetery, Strathmore Street, c. 1910. The cemetery lodge and gateposts can be seen with the Convalescent Home in the background. Barnhill cemetery was opened in 1869 following the closure of the Old Burial Ground at Chapel Lane, off Fisher Street, partly due to a cholera epidemic in 1866. Within Barnhill ~Cemetrey stands the Gilroy Mausoleum erected for George Gilroy (1815 –1892). The grand Tudor design of the mausoleum reflects the style and grandeur of Castleroy.

Convalescent Home, Barnhill, near Broughty Ferry.

Dundee Convalescent Home, 31 Strathmore Street, *c.* 1906. The Convalescent Home was founded in 1876 with funds left by Sir David Baxter (1793-1872). David Baxter rose to the position of principal partner in the linen manufactures, Baxter Brothers, Dens Works, Dundee. The Home, under the management of Dundee Royal Infirmary, had space for eighty-four patients. Admission was obtained by the presentation of a recommendation from a Dundee Medical Practitioner to the Medical Superintendent at the Infirmary. In 1891 patients included spinners and weavers from Dundee's textile mills.

Dundee Convalecent Home, *c.* 1930. On 9 September 1863 David Baxter, together with his sisters, donated Baxter Park to the citizens of Dundee in memory of their father. William Baxter. The park was designed and laid out by Sir Joseph Paxton, creator of Crystal Palace, London. David Baxter was knighted by the Queen in 1863 in recognition of his position in the linen industry and his benefaction of Baxter Park. Sir David was also presented with a statue of himself that stands outside the Albert Institute, Dundee.

Soldiers, Dundee Convalescent Home, c. 1916. Nineteen soldiers together with their officer are seen with the matron and housekeeper at the entrance of the convalescent home. The home was used for troop accommodation during the First World War. On the reverse of the card Sergeant J. Hardie states that the weather was bad with snow waist deep. The men had to participate in route marches every day in full marching order. After the home was demolished, the site was acquired by the East of Scotland Housing Association Ltd in 1971 with assistance from the Dundee Corporation.

French postcard from the front, May 1916. The card was sent by a nurse at No.12 Casualty Clearing Station, whilst on active service with the British Expeditionary Force in France. The writer shows appreciation for the tulips, perhaps a gift from Mrs Watson, Rhona Place, BF. The crossing to Boulogne was described as rough but safe. The message, quite uncommitted in its contents, was passed by the field censor and cancelled in red with a hexagonal stamp.

Linlathern House, *c.* 1880. Linlathern House was built for David Graham in 1705. When David Graham died around 1728, the house was passed to his eldest son, Robert. When Robert died in 1756, his eldest son, also called Robert, inherited his estate. Robert was a Commissioner of Excise and friend of Robert Burns. It was through this association that Robert Burns found employment as an excise officer and thus enhanced his career prospects. When Robert Graham sold his estate it came into the possession of David Erskine, a successful lawyer.

Linlathern Den, 1903, David Erskine died on 5 April 1791. In 1803 the Linlathern estate was passed on to his son, James. In 1811 James married his cousin Katherine Stirling and they took up residence at Linlathern House. The couple had four children but they all died within a few days of birth. In 1816 James Erskine, aged 28 years, died. James's brother Thomas succeeded in ownership and extended the house around 1830. Thomas Erskine, a local benefactor, never married and died in 1870. A later occupant was David Erskine, liberal MP for West Perthshire (1906-9).

East Bridge over Dichty Burn, Linlathern Estate, *c.* 1905. Linlathern House and the steading dated 1770 were finally demolished in the 1980s. However the cast and wrought iron estate road bridge built around 1795 to 1810 still survives. The bridge was built to give independent access to the steading, avoiding the drives to Linlathern House. The bridge is the oldest iron bridge in Scotland and is amongst the oldest in the world.

The Wishing Well, Balmossie Den, *c.* 1911. Fintry Bridge spans the eastern entrance to the grounds of Linlathern House. On the bank of the Dighty Burn stands a Wishing Well. A stone at the site of the well is inscribed 'Whosoever drinketh of the water shall thirst again T.E. 1847.' Thomas Erskine had the stone erected on the supposed site of a medieval holy well.

Select Bibliography

Boase, MM; *I Stir the Poppy Dust* (Innes J and G, Ltd, 1936)

Brotchie, AW; *Tramways of the Tay Valley* (Dundee Museums and Art Galleries, 1965)

Brotchie, AW and Herd, JJ; *Old Broughty Ferry and Monifieth* (N.B. Traction Group, 1980)

Crampsay, RA; *The King's Grocer: The Life of Sir Thomas Lipton* (Glasgow City Libraries 1996)

Cronshaw, A; *Old Dundee Picture Postcards* (Mainstream Publishing Co. Ltd, 1988)

Cronshaw, A; *JB White of Dundee. Picture Postcard Monthly* (Reflections of a Bygone age, October 1994)

Cronshaw, A; *Topographical Postcards of Dundee – Part 2. Picture Postcard Monthly* (Reflections of a Bygone Age, January 1995)

Cronshaw, A; *R.H. Lundie, Dundee's nonagerarian stationer and postcard publisher. Picture Postcard Monthly* (Reflections of a Bygone Age, February 1996)

Cronshaw, A; *Four Million postcards a month!* A history of Rotary Photographic Co. Ltd, West Drayton, Middlesex – Part 1. *Picture Postcard Monthly* (Reflections of a Bygone Age, April 1997)

Davey, N and Perkins, J; *Broughty Ferry, Village to Suburb* (Dundee Museums and Art Galleries, 1976)

Dundee Directory (Mathew, JP and Co, various dates)

Grove Academy Centenary Issue (1889 –1989) *School Magazine* (Grove Academy, 1989)

Lansdell, A; *History in Camera – Seaside Fashions 1860 – 1939* (Shire Publications, 1990)

Malcolm, J; *The Parish of Monifieth in Ancient and Modern Times* (Green W. and Sons, 1910)

McKean, C and Walker, D; *Dundee: An Illustrated Architectural Guide* (RIAS, 1993)

Millar, AH; *Glimpses of Old and New Dundee* (MacLeod, 1925)

Perkins, J; *Steam Trains to Dundee 1831-1863* (Dundee Museums and Art Galleries, 1975)

St Margaret's Barnhill (1884 – 1984) Centenary Pictorial Booklet Church and Parish (St Margaret's Church, 1984)

Watson, M; *Jute and Flax Mills in Dundee* (Hutton Press Ltd, 1990)

Watt, G; *The Story of St Margaret's Church, Barnhill, Dundee, 1884 – 1984* (St Margaret's Church, 1984)